WHAT'S IN YOUR SURNAME?

WILLIAM LEWIS

WHAT'S IN YOUR SURNAME?

THE FASCINATING STORY OF BRITISH SURNAMES

BRAZEN HEAD PUBLISHING
Abingdon

Brazen Head Publishing · PO Box 584 · Abingdon · Oxfordshire · OX14 9FL

www.brazenheadpublishing.co.uk

Published in the United Kingdom
by Brazen Head Publishing

First published 2010

A catalogue record for this book is available from the British Library

ISBN 978-0-9565106-0-0

This book is dedicated with great affection
to my daughters, Maggie and Kate.

ACKNOWLEDGEMENTS

My special thanks are due to John Day, whose advice and help with the planning and presentation of this book have been invaluable to a word–processing novice; also my gratitude is due to Jackie Osborne and Javier Fernandez for their expertise and patience in nursing my limited understanding of computer technique.

CONTENTS

Preface

I think that most people would agree that of all our possessions (next to life itself) our names are our most personal and special. We are so used to them that we rarely give them a thought in the general course of things. Because we hear our first names (or 'given' names, as they are sometimes called) from our very earliest years, these soon become firmly rooted in our minds, to be joined a little later by our surnames ('family' names). Before long, both names emerge automatically whenever occasion demands, sometimes several times a day. We write them and speak them without thinking about them and we respond to our names instantly when we hear them spoken. So important have personal names become to us that we have an irresistible urge to bestow names upon many of our possessions – our cats, dogs, goldfish and other pets, our houses, dolls and teddy bears; our motorcars, boats, aircraft and trains; even space-craft are given evocative names.

There is clearly a powerful mechanism behind all this naming, for its roots must lie in the earliest times when our remote, newly human ancestors began to feel the need to use sounds to identify each other and to name objects around them.

Having just remarked that we usually pay little attention to our names, it is nevertheless true that most of us think about our surnames sometimes, though we may not know anything about their origins, unless they speak clearly for themselves, like **Baker**, **Robertson**, **Lancaster** and **Smallbone**. Such names as these clearly suggest their meanings and therefore hint at their origins. However, it won't take us long to think of some common surnames whose meanings seem far from clear and even very puzzling indeed: how about **Lloyd**, **Wray**, **Latimer**, **Winterbottom** and **Clegg**, for instance? These are fairly familiar surnames, but what are they hiding from us?

I think most of us realise that, with so many different and descriptive surnames in use, there must be some good historical reasons for their adoption. The first four surnames in the previous paragraph,

Baker, **Robertson**, **Lancaster** and **Smallbone**, give us the first clue: these surnames seem to suggest an occupation, a relationship, a place and a physical characteristic, in that order and, as with many surnames, neither their spellings, nor their meanings have altered very much over the centuries. However, there are many words that *have* undergone changes of meaning or spelling (or both), while some of the surnames that we are familiar with today, come from words which have long since vanished from use, with the result that many surnames' histories remain obscured in the dense mists of mediæval time. Even so, it is still true that every surname has a history and an interesting story to tell, a story that may even reach back to a time long before the Norman Conquest of England in the middle of the 11th century. In many cases, however, it was during the 11th and 12th centuries that we notice the first occasional instances of *written* British surnames – of a sort.

It will take many years yet for every surname in current use to receive attention, for it is very time-consuming work for both scholars and amateurs who, for the pure love of their subject, diligently examine thousands of records from many hundreds of sources.

Those people who are lucky enough to possess an unusual surname, need never feel ill-at-ease (though they sometimes do) amongst the Smiths, the Taylors, the Webbs, the Vincents and the Jacksons: indeed, far from it. Such familiar surnames as these are usually the extroverts who boldly announce their descent to the world, while intriguing surnames like **Atter**, **Belcher**, **Sleggs**, **Stelfox**, **Possee** and thousands more, prefer to keep themselves to themselves – sometimes very successfully indeed.

From our earliest childhood, we are made aware of our names: our parents ensure that we respond to our names as soon as possible, so that a deep and indelible identity is established in our minds without delay. First we learn to respond to our forenames and then, as time goes on, our surnames become tightly bound to the personal name and it is during these early years that the seeds of the life to come take deepest root, our own identity perhaps having the deepest root of all. Our names are one expression of that identity.

Soon we become aware that other people have names too and, quite unconsciously, begin the process of 'categorizing' them. This seems eventually to involve placing the surnames we hear against a fanciful scale like this:

Neutral names   Strange names   Bizarre names

This scale, which shows how names can vary in their appeal to us, runs from neutral-type names, like **Smith**, **Jones**, **Jackson** and **Brooks**, through strange sounding names, such as **Cathcart**, **Fawcett**, **Tumber** and

Simmonite, to the apparently bizarre ones, like **Longbottom, Smellie, Raghip** and **Gotobed**.

I should think there would be general agreement about roughly where on the scale we would place a given surname. Those names at the left hand side of the scale tend to be universally acceptable (and sometimes envied) and rarely draw forth comment or attract attention to themselves. The names near the middle usually set us thinking and wondering, in a general sort of way, about the possible reasons for such words' becoming surnames. Their sounds and perhaps their images in our minds are more striking than the neutral types. Those surnames at the right hand end of the scale are least appreciated because they often sound amusing or produce a humorous picture (usually quite false) in our minds. Those people whose surnames belong to this end sometimes wish for a name from the other end (and sometimes change their names accordingly!) The apparently humorous nature of many names at the right hand end of our scale is the result of their being judged at their modern face value, whereas their real or original meanings will usually give a very different picture. As I said earlier, possessors of unusual surnames should try not to feel self-conscious about them, though this feeling is entirely understandable, especially when such names are a constant source of tiresome joking. Possessors of the surnames **Mudd**, **Crapper**, **Thicke** and **Goodbody** will know what I mean. (I once read of a man who, following an acrimonious divorce, is said to have changed his name from **Lovelady** to **Hayter**. On the face of it, he seems to have made his point!)

No book about surnames can include more than a very small fraction of names in current use. In this study I will tell the story of how names came into being, together with the histories and meanings of a good number of them, both familiar and unfamiliar. An essential aid to my work has been the London telephone directory, which I have repeatedly used as an initial check on both the existence and frequency of almost all the surnames mentioned in the text. On many occasions too, I have consulted every other mainland UK telephone book, as well as the national electoral registers in an effort to establish the likelihood of survival of certain names (**Wednesday**, **Juggler** and **October** are examples). The fact that a name does not appear in any telephone directory does not mean of course, that it has become extinct; there are many 'ex-directory' numbers and not everyone has a telephone anyway. The surname may also survive in the United States, Australia or New Zealand, for example. The internet too, has become a useful tool in locating names.

Although there remains a vast amount of work still to be done in the field of surname research, there have been, over the years, several very distinguished scholars whose research and dedication have contributed enormously to our understanding of the evolution of our surnames.

One of the earliest to publish a study and commentary on the origins and usage of names, both forenames and surnames, was William Camden (1551-1623). His book, 'Britannia', was enormously successful for the time and ran to at least six editions before 1607. Camden was a learned historian, teacher and antiquary, who was a keen observer of the English people and who had closely studied many of the written records that were available to him, including Domesday Book. Although Camden devoted only a single chapter in his book to surnames, he included a detailed description of the origins of names generally, the history of British surnames, their forms and their meanings, covering well over two thousand names in the process, while revealing to us his charming Elizabethan literary style and wit.

It is interesting to remember that Camden lived and worked in Westminster at precisely the time that his great contemporary and exponent of the English language, William Shakespeare, was acting and writing plays in nearby Southwark and Blackfriars.

Since Camden's day, there have been many studies made and many volumes written on the history of British surnames and, of the scholars in the centuries after William Camden, perhaps the two most notably pioneering were Canon C.W. Bardsley in the 19th century and Dr P.H. Reaney in the 20th. Indeed, Dr Reaney's great Dictionary remains in print and is a major source of information to students of surnames. However, as there are relatively few other books about surnames in print, I hope that you, the reader, will find this one a book which, either may be read comfortably from beginning to end, or else may be dipped into as the fancy takes you and that it will give you as much pleasure to read as it gave me to write.

William Lewis
Oxford, December 2009.

.

Chapter 1

What are surnames and how old are they?

Everyone knows that their surname is their family name, the name that has been inherited, usually through their fathers and which has been passed down through many generations over hundreds of years. So what exactly is a surname?

The prefix 'sur-' derives originally from the Latin 'super', and comes to us via the French word 'sur', both of which mean 'on, above or over', and which suggest that a surname is an extra name, over and above the personal first name. Indeed, in French, the word 'surnom' means 'nickname', which is certainly an extra name.

The Romans

All our surnames began as nicknames of some sort, but we have to thank the Ancient Romans for the idea of adding a descriptive after-name to the personal name, for they developed a system of naming which was both simple and logical (as we would expect), but its application was reserved almost solely for the male citizen-class and above. Slaves would have only a single name, but three names would usually be assigned to the male children of the citizen classes (occasionally a fourth and even a fifth name may be encountered). The first name was known as the 'praenomen' and was simply a forename, for example Gaius, Marcus, Augustus and Lucius are well-known Roman male first names or 'praenomina'. However, these forenames appear to have been little used except on formal occasions.

The second of the three names was the 'nomen' and identified the family or tribe into which the boy was born. Maccius, Julius and Annaeus are examples of 'nomina'.

The third name to be given was known as the 'cognomen' and was purely descriptive. These 'cognomina' were sometimes harshly accurate (if not a little cruel) in their portrayals of their bearers: Flaccus ('flap-eared'), Claudius ('cripple'), Varus ('knock-kneed') and Brutus ('heavy, stupid') were some fairly descriptive ones. It will seem rather puzzling to us that the practice of applying unflattering names to their male children persisted for so long amongst the Roman citizen classes.

A fourth name was likely to have been an inherited name, while a fifth name would have been awarded in recognition of a great deed such as leading the victory over an enemy. These names were referred to as 'agnomina'.

Girls were usually given a single name, which was often a feminised version of a male name: Julia, Flavia, Cornelia and Aurelia are easily recognised examples. However, in spite of over four hundred years of occupation of Britain, the Roman system of conferring names made no permanent impression on the native Britons, many of whom must have become familiar with the Latin language spoken by the local Roman occupiers. We must therefore wonder just how complete was the Roman cultural conquest of the country: the real extent of 'Romanisation' of these islands can only be surmised. In any case, the natives of these shores were to come under the powerful influence of a series of further occupations after the withdrawal of the Romans at the beginning of the 5th century and must quickly have begun to lose any Romish ways they had acquired. It is still the case, however, that intermarriage between the native Britons and the Roman occupiers has left us with a significant number of surnames derived from the Latin: **Clements**, **Vincent** and **Patrick** are well known surnames today, but who would guess that **Joll** and **Jullings** are of Roman origin too? These are simply variations on the name (the 'nomen') Julius.

After the Romans

Sometime during the year AD 410, the last of the Roman legions had abandoned Britain, leaving the defence and government of these islands in the hands of the native inhabitants. Over the next four hundred years, England would fall prey to a series of invasions: the Picts and Scots in the north, the Irish in the west, the Jutes from Denmark in Kent and the Angles and Saxons from Germany in the east (and later, the Midlands). By the late 9th century, the Danes too, had established themselves in the north-east. However, it was to be the Normans, themselves of Scandinavian decent, led by Duke William from the north-east of France, who would defeat the English near Hastings in October 1066 and who would have the greatest and most enduring effect on English society.

The impact of the invading Saxons (beginning in the 5th century) on the native language of England and therefore on our surnames, was to be much greater than that of the later Danes, whose contribution has been much more in evidence in our place-names (especially in the north-east of England, the part called 'Danelaw' – see the map on page 55.) Of course, place-names have themselves, played a vital role in British surname formation: we can all think of someone whose surname is also a place-name. In this way, the 9th century Danish settlers have furnished us with an important element in our surname development. The tell-tale suffix '-by' (meaning 'settlement') will nearly always indicate a place name of Danish origin: **Enderby** (Leicestershire), meant Endri-othi's settlement and **Danby** (North Yorkshire) was simply 'the Danes' settlement'. The equivalent Saxon suffix was '-tun', giving rise to places ending with '-ton', such as **Langton** ('long village').

If we now look at the names of some of the kings and high ranking nobles in the two centuries before the Conquest (that is in the 9th and 10th centuries), we will notice that their admiring contemporaries had already begun to add an extra name describing some feature of character or conduct:

Alfred the Great (1149-1199);
Edmund Ironside (981-1016);
Harold Harefoot (died 1040);
Siward the Valiant (11th century).

Some other notables, however, acquired nicknames that reflected characteristics other than battle prowess:

Edward the Martyr (c.963-978);
Ethelred the Unready (968-1016 and meaning 'lacking wisdom');
Edward the Confessor (1002-1066).

Others simply bore the names of their kingdoms:

Egbert of Wessex (9th century);
Edwy of Essex (died 959);
Guthfrith of Northumbria (10th century).

It was about the year AD1000 that some French nobles began to adopt a form of after-name, deliberately chosen to recall those races and lands that they had lately subjugated. Since the English King Edward ('the Confessor') was, in the words of the 17th century antiquary, William Camden, 'all Frenchified', it may be that the idea of an additional descriptive name had arrived in England some time before the Norman Conquest of 1066. It was, however, the arrival of the Norman occupiers that provided the real impetus and laid the foundations for the English surname revolution.

England under the Normans

Native English peasants had no need whatever of a functional second name (or 'by-name'), but we know from ancient written records that men sometimes acquired a spoken nickname after their personal name. These after-names were entirely incidental, however, and died with their bearers, there being no reason to pass on the nickname. This casual and informal oral custom might well have persisted for much longer were it not for the demands of post-Conquest recording systems that were needed for the purposes of taxation, wills, deeds and court records. Norman officialdom required accurate identification of individuals and as a consequence, there were many cumbersome descriptions which accompanied a personal name: 'Alexandro filio Willelmi Saundr'[1] and 'Willelmo ad capud ville'[2] are two instances from the early 14th century, which show that even by this late stage, there must have been many individuals who still lacked a fixed surname.

The clerks, most of whom were Norman in the decades following the Conquest, had to do their best to write down the unfamiliar sounds uttered by the English peasants and it is hardly a surprise to find that there are many variations of spelling of similar words and names. Few names today have retained the exact spellings first set down by those 11th and 12th century scribes.

We can learn something of the state of Norman thinking on this subject in the late 11th century, by examining some of the entries in Domesday Book. This great work (there are two volumes: Great and Little Domesday) is the result of a vast survey commissioned by King William and carried out in the first half of 1086, by means of which the King could determine both the taxable value of his English possessions and their current military capability. As a result, only the principal landholders and those who held property from them as tenants are mentioned by name. Unfortunately, the rest of the population was simply counted. The names of some of the important tenants in the borough of Oxford are revealing:

Henry de Ferrers, William Peverell, Edward the Sheriff, Arnulf de Hesdin, Berengar de Tosny, Milo Crispin, Richard de Courcy, Robert d'Oilly, Ranulf Flambard, Guy de Raimbeaucourt, Walter Giffard …

By stating where a man came from, he could be clearly and almost unambiguously identified. Six men in the Oxford list show their, or their families', places of origin by the inclusion of 'de' or 'd'. It is easy to see that Henry de Ferrers (a town in Normandy) is only one step away from

---

1. Subsidy Roll (1305–6 and 1327), Wheatley Records (Oxon.) – W. Hassall.
2. Ibid.

becoming known as Henry Ferrers by his neighbours. The same would be true of Richard de Courcy and indeed, these two names, **Ferrers** and **de Courcy** are modern English surnames, found in small numbers mostly in the southernmost counties.

A few men in the list above seem to have what look like true surnames already: William **Peverell**, Milo **Crispin**, Ranulf **Flambard** and Walter **Giffard**. These 'surnames' are actually derived from Norman nicknames, meaning respectively, 'peppery' (in temperament, perhaps), 'crinkled' (hair or beard), 'flaming torch' (strikingly red hair perhaps), and 'chubby-cheeked'.

The odd-man-out seems to be Edward the Sheriff. The personal name Edward is a Saxon name and he was almost certainly a native Englishman who, by the time of the Domesday survey, had achieved the high rank of sheriff and who held (we are told) two dwellings in the city of Oxford. There are over 50 entries of the surname **Sheriff** in the London telephone directory, which indicate that this surname is a strong survivor.

Later in the same section of the Domesday Oxford survey, we find listed the smaller landholders who, as we might expect, are mostly of English birth and bear familiar Saxon personal names. Here are some from the list:

Colman, Wulfwy the fisherman, William, Alwyn, Alric, Leofeva, Smewin, Edith, Suetman, Alwin the priest, Alwin, Suetman the moneyer, Godwin, another Suetman, Alwin ......

These more lowly individuals, some of whom are women, are given no additional names, apart from the occasional occupational description. However, we now begin to see the problem of ambiguity, which faced the king's commissioners and clerks: the name Alwin appears four times, but only one receives an additional designation (as a priest). This situation could obviously lead to confusion, as we have seen and long-winded descriptions were often added to a personal name to avoid misunderstandings.

On the extensive lands within Oxfordshire that were held by the Bishop of Lincoln, there lived about 766 peasants, variously described as 'slaves', 'villagers' and 'smallholders', but alas their names and nicknames and their specific occupations are not recorded and thus it was in the rest of the great survey. What a fascinating study it would have made, if the king's clerks had registered everyone's name.

So we now know that by the year 1087, Normans living in England were frequently accorded a sort of surname, most often denoting their town of origin in Normandy, while the native English were unaccustomed to the idea of an additional name, unless it were a descriptive nickname: Wulfwy the fisherman or Alwin the priest in the examples above. By the beginning of the 12th century, however, there was an increasing desire for greater administrative accuracy and this gave rise to such entries into official documents as, 'William the miller', 'William at well', 'William son of Richard' and 'William of red hair'. Such simple personal descriptions soon began to stick and were quickly shortened by the common folk to William Miller, William Atwell, William Richardson and William Redhead. Several local Williams could now be distinguished from each other by the use of a descriptive nickname.

Nicknames were applied to women too – we read of Edith Swanneck and Agnes Lickfinger – but most often, women were called after their husbands or fathers in official records: 'Matilda wyf of Robert Stronge', 'Johanna Robyndoghter', 'Agnes widow of Adam Wyte' and 'Juliana Williamwyf' are actual examples[1].

It was not uncommon for a person to be known by different names at different times. In a record dated 1395, we read of 'Nicholas Paynter, also known as Nichols Neuman ....'[2] and as late as 1418, we encounter 'Nicol Wigh, known as Nicholas Ketringham, also known as Nicol Pecche, also called John Seagrave....'[3] It is possible that there was nothing sinister in this: we meet the same thing today – authors and actors often use different names on different occasions and for quite legitimate reasons.

To summarise then: after a slow start, there was a noticeable increase in the rate of adoption of an additional name within the population until, by the middle of the 14th century, most Englishmen had acquired a permanent surname, which had at last become hereditary. This finally rounded off a process that had begun with nicknames accorded to those 9th and 10th century kings and noblemen.

Welsh surnames were to come later still, but the names of the Scots owe their origins to a rather different process of formation, as I shall describe in Chapter Five.

The different classes of surnames

As we have already discovered, surnames arose as nicknames of some sort, describing a feature of a person: size, shape, colour of skin or hair, a deformity, some aspect of behaviour, where he lived, where he came from, his occupation or a relationship to someone (usually his father). Scholars have long used this simple idea to classify surnames. Thus our surnames can be arranged into four major groups, with two important

---

1. P. H. Reaney The Origin of English Surnames. Routledge & Keegan Paul, 1979 edition.

2. Ibid.

3. P. H. Reaney The Origin of English Surnames. Routledge & Keegan Paul, 1979 edition.

sub-groups:

(i)   Surnames originating from an occupation, craft or office.
(ii)   (a) Surnames specifying a place of origin: village, town or shire.
        (b) Surnames from a local feature.
(iii)   Surnames from relationships.
(iv)   (a) Surnames from nicknames.
        (b) Surnames from personal names (including from saints' names &
        Biblical names).

The order of the groups above is simply that in which I have chosen to treat the subject and does not represent an order of importance or any recognised sequence of surname formation.

If these groups were all-embracing, we would have no difficulty at all in fitting every surname tidily into its unique category. Of course, many surnames are straightforward in this respect: **Mason**, **Dudley**, **Hill**, **Peterson**, **Short** and **James** all fit neatly into the groups shown above, beginning at the top. However, there are countless examples of surnames which could belong to two or even three groups. **Pye** is such an example, encompassing three groups: occupation, local feature and nickname and is a name which I will discuss in more detail in Chapter Two. A record-holder in the multiple category stakes must surely be **Beck**, which can boast five alternative sources and can occur in every group shown above, except in group 3 (names from relationships).

To give every possible origin of the surnames appearing in this book is an impossible task, so the reader should not be content with the opinions of a single authority, but search out all available references and commentaries on a particular surname, remembering that there are still a great many English surnames that have yet to be investigated and defined. With the increasing amount of archive detail accessible on the Internet, the fascinating task of investigating surnames, particularly their frequency, distribution and the likelihood of their survival is made very much easier than only a decade ago.

Chapter 2

Surnames from Occupations

THE VILLAGE

At the time when surnames in England were making their first hesitant appearances during the 12th century, the vast majority of English men and women were village dwellers, tied to the land on which they would work with their ploughs and scythes throughout their whole lives. The populations of towns and cities were minute when compared to those of today: Norwich, England's third largest town at the time of the Conquest, contained about 1300 dwellings, while Domesday credits Canterbury with only 250. Even at the beginning of the 15th century, there were probably no more than five towns having 1200 households or more: London, York, Coventry, Bristol and Norwich. Most mediæval towns were no bigger than today's large villages and many town dwellers tended their fields and meadows outside the town boundaries in the same way that the villagers tended theirs, reaping harvests and selling any small surplus in the town market.

At the end of the 11th century, the total population of England was about 1½ million, of which something over 90% were peasants who were bound to their lord. The lord himself would have held land from a greater lord, or from the Church, or directly from the King, who demanded certain services of labour from his subjects. Those commoners who were exempted from such services by reason of wealth or social standing, were known as 'freemen' and this title is recalled in the surname **Freeman**. However, since most men were villeins (that is, peasants), such a lowly status was hardly worth recording and so, although the surnames **Villan** and **Villin** are to be found today, they are very rare indeed, 3 of each currently cropping up in the Yorkshire telephone books. The modern English word 'villain' is commonly used today, of course (with modified meaning), as a term of contempt, indicating a low, roguish type. An alternative word for a peasant, frequently used in mediæval times was 'serf' and may be the indirect ancestor of our rather rare surname **Sarver**.

Some peasants had no access to fields in which to grow their own crops, indeed they possessed only the meanest of personal effects, usually living in hovels and had to labour for other villeins in order to scrape the most meagre existence. These poorest of the villagers must belong to that category which Domesday usually terms 'servi' – slaves. In some areas, these 'servi' were known as 'cotters'. If the 'cotters' represented the lowest social class in a village, the middle classes were represented by the freemen, who included the franklins and the husbandmen (or 'husbonds'). Each of these held a small acreage of his own and could support a household and a family. Of the freemen, the franklins formed a small, but higher-ranking class of their own. They owned and farmed a moderate acreage and were accorded appropriate privileges by their lord, such as exemption from military service. It is not surprising therefore, that such a social position gave rise to the surname **Franklin**. In the London telephone directory, the surname **Freeman** occurs no fewer than 720 times, outstripping **Franklin** by almost 2 to 1, reflecting the fact that not all freemen were of franklin status. The husbandman, who, like the franklin, owned both his own house and a small acreage, though was of lower social rank, has also left his mark on our surnames in the form of **Husband**, **Bond** and its less common form **Bundy**.

English mediæval villages, of course, came in many sizes – from the thousands of hamlets, each having only a handful of dwellings, to the much more substantial settlements containing several dozens. Nevertheless, most villages of more than a dozen or so habitations would conform to one of three natural patterns. The first and perhaps most natural, is the 'nucleated' village, which has its tenements gathered round a green or at a crossroads. In the second type, the houses are strung for some distance, ribbon-like, along one or both sides of the main thoroughfare. In the third, and rarer type, the habitations are scattered, often back from the street and the village lacks a recognisable centre. Marsh Baldon in Oxfordshire is a well-preserved example of the 'nucleated' village and Combe Martin in Devon illustrates the 'ribbon' pattern. The third type can be seen in the village of Peatling in Leicestershire. A man who lived hard by the green of his village, might well attract the nickname **Green**, while he whose dwelling was at the far end of the ribbon of cottages, might be called **Way** or **Lane**.

The larger villages would usually boast a greater variety of craftsmen than would the smaller settlements and it is from these artisans that most of the surnames in this chapter arise. Indeed there are many hundreds of names which are derived from the work done by peasants in and around their villages – far too many to mention. So we must be content to extract the principal ones from those that have come down to us.

The Miller

Domesday lists nearly 6000 mills throughout England for grinding corn into flour. These were all watermills, though not every village had access to a mill. Those without this valuable resource retained the hand-querning method of extracting the flour. Where a mill had been established, it was in the charge of a tenant **Miller**, who was entitled to collect about one-sixteenth of the flour he milled in payment for his service. Millers, however, were sometimes guilty of taking more than their due – Chaucer's miller took three times his entitlement. The mill was usually built by the lord, who forbade his subjects to use their own hand-querns (thereby avoiding the lord's fee). It is to be expected, therefore, that the miller's craft has given rise to a notable surname, which must be one of the record holders in the variations of spelling to be found. I have found twenty-seven versions in just a few minutes in the London telephone directory and there are several other variants less frequently encountered. Here are some of the more commonly found ones, most of which will be familiar to the reader: **Milard, Millin, Millinder, Mulliner, Mills, Milne, Milner, Milward, Molin, Mullard**. In the more central parts of England, the miller was often referred to as the **Bolter** or **Boulter**, peasants preferring the word 'bolt' (or 'boult') to the word 'mill' and which meant 'to sift or sieve'. There was one, Roger le Boleter, at work in the village of Osney, near Oxford, in 1246[1] and it is believed that he was the village miller – his name certainly suggests it was so. We are left to wonder whether any of his children continued in their father's craft of milling and whether one of them retained the title of 'le Boleter'. Perhaps some of the present day **Bolter**s or **Boulter**s in Oxford are descended from Roger, the 13th century Osney miller. Having said that, I must make the point that a 'bolter' was also a maker of 'bolts', those short darts that were fired from the crossbow. However, this particular craft was always a good deal less common than that of the miller, though the dart maker must take some small share of the credit for the formation of the surname.

The Smiths

Many villages possessed a worker in metal whose craft largely freed him from the regular land labour of his fellows and who received payments in cash or in goods for his services. This man was, of course the **Smith** (or smið as it would have been written. The letter ð was a useful symbol giving the soft '-th' sound, as in 'smith'. Another useful, though long

1. P. H. Reaney (1976) A Dictionary of British Surnames. Routledge & Keegan Paul.

abolished letter was Þ, which also stood for '-th', but this time in its voiced form, as in 'they'. The capital letter in both cases was Ð).

Today we usually associate the smith's work only with the making of horseshoes, but in mediæval times the **Smith** was a skilled and busy general iron-worker, concerned largely with the making, repairing and sharpening of tools and implements: pots, pans, blades, ploughshares, horse gear and so forth. That the surname **Smith** has become the most common of English surnames is not surprising, as we shall now see.

In towns, the smiths tended to develop special skills, as is clear from the variety of surnames that their distinct specialisms have handed down to us. A smith who could turn out good iron arrowheads when called upon, might soon become known as the **Arrowsmith**, while a specialist in horseshoe making would have been the **Shoesmith**. The nail maker and the knife maker are both credited with the name **Naismith**, while keys and locks were made by the **Locksmith**, a remarkably rare surname today.

Some metalsmiths focused their expertise on working particular metals: the **Blacksmith** concerned himself with the large variety of iron-ware in constant demand (perhaps surprisingly, **Blacksmith** is a very rare surname today); **Goldsmith** and **Whitesmith** will be discussed in *Work in the Town* later in the chapter.

An interesting statistic to end this discussion on the smiths is that there are about 1½ million bearers of the name **Smith** (not forgetting **Smyth** and **Smythe**) in Britain today. How many are there, one wonders, in the English-speaking world?

Some Other Indoor Occupations

At this point, I think it will be helpful to mention that there are several useful clues that are often suggestive of a surname derived from an occupation or craft. The suffixes -ar, -er, -or, -ard and -art are such indicators, though not all names with these endings are of occupational origin – **Bart**, for example, is an abbreviation of the personal name **Bartholomew** and **Winter** is of course a seasonal name. The occasional suffix '-man', as well as '-wright', from the Old English 'wrytha', are also signs to look out for in the identification of occupational surnames. However, most of the names we shall encounter in the rest of this section will belong to the first mentioned group.

Let's begin with **Baker**, currently the fourth most common English surname. This tradesman was an important member of many a village community, for he was usually the only one permitted by the lord to bake bread. Like the miller, the baker was often suspected of trickery by taking more than his due, or mixing chalk with the dough after a concealed accomplice had removed a quantity from beneath the kneading board. Bakers in towns were probably more guilty of such malpractices than the village bakers. This trade has also given us the surname **Baxter**. This was originally the feminine form of **Baker**, but soon came to be used for both sexes, as did a number of similar words, which we shall meet in due course.

Some of the larger villages had a tailor too, but most of the peasant women could make the simple clothes worn by everyone in their families. **Taylor** (this is the original spelling) is the second most common English surname at the present time.

An industry which grew in importance throughout the middle ages was that of weaving. This craft has provided us with many surnames, the most common of which is **Webb** (which is currently the fifth most common English surname). Two well-known variations on this name are **Webber** and **Webster**, which once again, illustrate the masculine and feminine forms. The London telephone directory reveals a prevalence of **Webster** over **Webber** by more than 2 to 1 (475 entries to 229). The thread spinners too, exhibited masculine and feminine forms: **Spinner** and **Spinster**. The first of these is still to be found as a rather uncommon surname, though it occurs with unexpected frequency around Canterbury and Thanet. With no family of her own to look after, an unmarried woman in mediæval England would expect to spend much of her time at her spinning and she may well have had to prepare the wool herself too. **Spinster**, as a surname, may be on the very edge of extinction, for I can locate only in mainland electoral records. The word spinster, as a legitimate means of describing an unmarried woman, has nowadays become unfashionable.

One who specialised in combing the raw wool became the **Comber** (though this name may also have referred to one who lived in a shallow valley or 'coomb'). The **Camer**, **Camber** and **Carder** probably did the same sort of job, perhaps even making the combs (or cards) with which to comb out the fleece. Once again, we find masculine and feminine variants of **Comber**, in the surnames **Kimber** (also found as **Kember**) and **Kempster**.

The general-purpose noun **Weaver** is further evidence of the growing importance of the mediæval cloth-making trade.

Newly woven cloth was stiff and coarse and needed to be softened before it was dyed. This process was called 'fulling' and was carried out by the **Fuller**, who beat and trampled the raw cloth in running water. **Voller** is a less common version of the same name. An unexpected surname in this context is **Walker**. The **Walker** also 'fulled' the cloth by 'walking' (that is trampling) it in water. In the south-west of England, the preference was for the word **Tucker**, 'tucking' having the same meaning as 'fulling'.

The newly 'fulled' cloth was then ready to be dyed. Woad, the once common English plant, was the source of a blue dye that was widely used by the **Dyer** (the original feminine form of which was **Dexter**). In the north of the country, the dyer was called the **Lister**. Although blue was probably the most commonly used colour in the mediæval cloth industry, other colours were prepared and those who produced them were sometimes known by particular names: the **Madder** made the red dye from the root of the madder plant, while the **Corker** extracted the purple dye from a lichen known as corkir.

From all of this it is clear that the cloth industry of mediæval England has been the source of a significant number of surnames and no wonder, it was an important 'growth industry', as we would say today. Wool was the most important raw material from which fabrics were made, far more so than flax which, though used, never gained the popularity of wool. It follows then, that such names as **Flax** and **Flaxman** – a worker with, or seller of flax – are far less common than the names associated with the wool industry. The arrival of cotton as a serious competitor of wool and its subsequent heyday, were several centuries in the future. The surname **Cotton** has no connection with the cloth trade, but referred to a dweller 'at the cottages'.

The Old English word 'wrytha' was originally applied to one who worked principally with wood and it is from this ancient word that we have the surname **Wright**. Like 'smith', it soon appeared as a suffix in its own right, describing a variety of skills involving the working of wood. The maker of wheels became the **Wheelwright**, though the shortened version **Wheeler** became a much more common surname in the end, as a glance at any telephone book will show – mine lists 201 **Wheelers**, but only a solitary **Wheelwright**. The **Plowright** made the wooden parts of ploughs (leaving the **Smith** to fashion the iron share), while the **Wainwright** (from the Old English 'waegn', a waggon) was a maker of waggons and the **Cartwright** constructed carts (waggons too, in all probability, when the need arose). Wooden chests (called 'arks') were useful for storing goods and were made by the **Arkwright**.

As time passed, the word 'wright' lost its specific woodworking reference and took on the more general meaning of 'maker'. Thus we have **Boatwright, Cheesewright** and **Sievewright** – a maker of sieves. There are others in this group, but they are rare. Indeed, many interesting and descriptive combinations have long since become extinct. Such names described makers of glass, laths, oars, baskets and casks among many more. However, a few of the '-wrights' we may encounter today are deceptive: **Goodwright** and **Allwright** are each found in appreciable numbers in our 'phone books, but are renderings of the Old English personal names Godric ('good-ruler') and Aethelric ('noble-ruler').

The conquering Normans brought with them a new word, 'carpentier', which was the French equivalent of the Old English 'wrytha' and has given us **Carpenter**. This word tended to replace 'wright' as a craftsman's designation, but it ultimately failed to supersede **Wright** as an English surname, as we shall see if we glance at our telephone directories: there are about five times more **Wrights** than **Carpenters**! However, the Normans introduced two other words from wood crafting which were soon adopted as surnames and are familiar to us today: **Joiner** and **Turner**. The **Joiner** (also frequently seen as **Joyner**) specialised in producing basic furniture, while the **Turner** fashioned bowls, dishes and the like on a simple lathe. Other vessels, such as jars and pots were the domain of the **Potter** (or **Potman** in some localities). This artisan was doubtless nicknamed **Potts** by his neighbours. General crockery was made and sold by the **Crocker** (now also found as **Croker**). These craftsmen would have been familiar faces at the weekly markets selling their wares in the nearby town.

An important constituent of every villager's diet was ale. Water was not to be trusted, for even eight hundred years ago, everyone recognised the dangers of drinking foul or tainted water, though many people of all social classes must have perished from typhoid, cholera, diarrhœa and a host of other water-borne diseases nonetheless. Ale provided the best alternative and was usually brewed by the women in their cottages during the autumn months. Those who made a living by selling their ale were naturally known as **Brewers** or **Brewsters** (here's that feminine form again). Often, the ale would be dispensed from large wooden casks by the **Tapper** or **Tapster** (feminine). Both **Tapper** and **Tapster** are not now common surnames, though I have located over a hundred instances of each, in electoral records countrywide. The maker of those wooden casks, however, has left us with his name in great numbers: he was the **Cooper** (**Cowper**, **Copper** and **Cupper** are alternative spellings). In some places he was called the **Tubman**.

Although the word 'barrel' is familiar enough to us today, it is a rather rare surname, which is perhaps a little surprising, since it was in use during the surname-forming period and is known to have been applied as an additional name in the middle of the 12th century. It was almost certainly used as an unflattering nickname for one who possessed a well-rounded belly. When found as a surname, it nearly always appears with a doubled final consonant, **Barrell**. There are currently three examples listed in my local 'phone book.

Some Outdoor Occupations

Many of the craftsmen I have mentioned so far must have worked for much of their time indoors, but it is from outdoor occupations that the majority of our occupational surnames have derived. Much of the work done around the village, though essential, was unskilled, so although the tasks themselves were common enough, they were not sufficiently notable, or there were too many people doing them to bring forth comment in the ordinary way of things. Almost any man could plough when the need arose, though some would do the job better than others of course and the ploughman was a familiar sight at autumn time. As a result, the surname **Plowman** is not very frequently met today (there being only 35 listed in the London telephone directory and 9 in my local directory). The same argument must apply to **Digweed**, a delightfully descriptive name you'll agree and of that general worker of the soil, the **Tiller**.

The **Osler**, another uncommon name, from the French 'oiseleur', was a bird catcher, but even small boys could learn to catch birds, while the bird scarer may have given us the name **Bugg** (and **Bugge**), from a word for scarecrow (but also see Chapter 7, *Nicknames from Insects* p.112). The natural rule seems to be, the more commonplace the job, the less likely it is to have produced a surname.

The peasants who worked the land for their lord were bound to him for life, according to established feudal law. Their lord, however, was not bound to one village. He would either have been granted the tenancy, by the king or by the Church, of a number of estates, divided by the Tenant-in-Chief into units known as manors, or else he may have inherited them from the original grantee. His estates and manors were almost always scattered throughout a large area of the realm, thus necessitating a great deal of travel as he made his rounds of inspection, wintering here, holding court there, sometimes remaining only a short time in one place before moving on to another district, perhaps for the hunting. Many of his subjects may never have seen their lord, especially if he held several dozens of estates throughout the kingdom. Since he could not supervise the management of each of his domains in person, he would appoint a manager of his affairs in each district. This important official was known as the **Bailiff**. In this form, this is a fairly rare surname today (I note only 1 in my local telephone directory, though there are nearly 200 in the current national electoral registers), but three of its variations are much more familiar: **Bailey** is by far the most common, with **Baylis(s)** and **Baly** coming next. In some areas the estate manager was called the **Granger** and in a few places, where the Norman influence was particularly marked, his title was the **Seneschal** (from an Old French word for a nobleman's chief household official). There are several variants of the name, including **Senskell**.

The villagers were required to elect their own foreman to work under the direction of the bailiff, supervising the work of the community, ensuring that every man did his fair share and calling men to work on the lord's own land (known as the demesne) two or three times a week. As the villager's representative, he would also pass on to the bailiff any complaints or disputes arising during the course of the day's labour. The name of this key officer was the **Reeve**, from the Old English 'gerefa'. This root also gives us the surnames **Greave** and **Greves**, among others. The reeve's job was often unpopular among the rest of the villagers, not least because he was exempted from manual labour and was granted certain other privileges which, in some cases, enabled him to become rather better off than the rest of the villeins and frequently resulted in a larger house. On his honesty, authority and judgment much of the prosperity and well-being of the village depended.

Under the **Reeve** was the **Hayward**, who was chiefly responsible for keeping the hedges in good order, so that grazing cattle, swine and other livestock did not wander into corn or onto other cultivated ground. Since he must bear the blame and take the consequences of damage caused by straying animals, the hayward's job was one of the least popular in the village and so it was held for only one year before another villager was elected to take his place.

Tending the animals was a full-time occupation in most cases and as a result, we find that sheep, pigs, goats and cattle have produced many surnames between them. The most familiar of them all is probably **Shepherd**, which is to be found in about ten different spellings and simply means the 'sheep herder'. There are several other surnames associated with sheep, among them **Lambert** (the lamb herder), **Ewart** (the ewe herder) and **Wetherhead** (the wether herder – a wether is a ram). **Lambkin**, however, meaning 'little lamb', may well have been an affectionate name for a child, rather than one who tended the lambs.

The mediæval pig, an animal rather different in appearance from our modern creature, was tended by the swineherd, which has become **Swinnart**, and the hog (the male pig or boar) was in the care of the hog herd, hence **Hoggart** and **Hogarth**. The cattle themselves, were watched over by the cowherd, **Coward**, who was sometimes called the **Cowman** (unusually, **Booth** too could signify one whose job was the care of the cattle, for it referred to the herdsman's hut), while the name **Calvert** derives from the 'calf herd'. Compared with the sheep, goats were of not much importance and surnames from this animal are less common. The ones most likely to be encountered are **Goater**, **Goatman** and **Gothard** (that is 'goat herd'). Geese were often kept for their eggs and meat and **Gozzard** ('goose herd') recalls the task.

The lord's stud horses were one of his most valuable assets and the man who looked after them was the 'stud herd', which has given us the name **Stoddart**. A name which breaks this pattern of spelling for these village occupations is **Steers**, which looks rather more like a nickname than a true occupational name because by now, we have become used to the -er, -ar, -ard and -art suffixes, as described earlier in this chapter. Steers were young oxen and **Steers** was their keeper.

There are other names that have come down to us from workers in the village, but they are only rarely encountered these days and at this point, I think we can take our leave of the land workers and animal keepers, in order to consider surnames arising from two other aspects of mediæval village life, the builders and the leather workers.

Although the peasants themselves would build and repair their own dwellings with whatever material was immediately available – a mixture of stone, wood, turf and mud were their usual materials – they would not be employed to do the more demanding work of repairing and maintaining the larger buildings, the Hall, the church and the large tithe barns. For this work, skilled artisans were required. Not every village of course, could boast a **Mason**, **Tyler** (also **Tiler**), **Slater** (or **Slatter**), or a **Thatcher** (and **Thacker**), but these crafts were common and such craftsmen would not be far away.

The villagers' cottages, being built largely of wood and thatch, were in constant peril of fire, especially in close-built communities, where a blaze could sweep through a whole street in a few minutes. Indeed, fires were so frequent in London, that regulations were issued in 1189 requiring citizens and builders to adopt stone for walls and tiles for roofs as safety measures. The **Tyler**, therefore, was a craftsman in increasing demand for roof work, while tiled floors were regarded as something of a luxury throughout the period.

Building stone walls for dwellings was the job of the **Waller** (though this surname has more than one origin), who was busier in and around the towns than in the villages, where such work was done mostly by the villagers themselves. The **Waller**'s modern day equivalent would be the bricklayer.

Our visit to the English mediæval village ends with a glance at the crafts of the leather workers. There was not a leather craftsman in every settlement by any means, but leather itself was plentiful and was always in demand for horse-gear, bottles, buckets, pouches, bags and shoes. The **Shoemaker** in the town was a considerable craftsman in this material, but peasants' footwear was cruder and cheaply made: both the soles and upper parts of their shoes were of a rather soft leather and would have worn out quickly. The specialist preparer of leather was the **Tanner**, who carried out a lengthy process, in which the hides were soaked in water with crushed oak bark obtained from the **Barker**. Bottles too, were often of leather before glass became widely available and their maker has given us the surnames **Bottell** and **Botler**.

As we leave the villagers, we might just glance back at the number of occupations and crafts that we have encountered which have conformed to the -ar, -er, -or, -art and -ard patterns. Out of the 66 occupational names I have mentioned, excluding all of the '-smiths' (8) and the '-wrights' (11), 48 follow the pattern (that is 73%) and a further 4 have retained the Old English suffix '-man' (which implies 'servant' or 'worker'). As we move away from the village community, we shall find that there are many more surnames of this type.

Work Beyond the Village

Though most of mediæval England's population lived in villages, we do find that there were individuals who lived or worked beyond the village boundary. These too, have left us with a few names, according to their occupations. Such outsiders were usually known to those living in the nearby settlements by some form of nickname, often describing their location, such as Henry **Longbottom**, meaning 'Henry in the long valley', or Ranulf **Underwood**, meaning 'Ranulf in the wood, or beneath the wooded hill'. Surnames derived from local features form a large group and will have Chapter Four to themselves.

Woods and forests were much more extensive in the middle ages than they are today. Woodland was exactly that, but forests were rather different. About a third of England, that is something like 16,000 square miles, was designated 'forest' at the beginning of the 13th century and included many moorlands, heaths and hundreds of villages with all their fields, greens, meadows and wastes. Since wood itself was a highly important building material as well as being the primary source of fuel, it is to the true woodland close to the village that we turn for our first crop of surnames. An obvious name that will come into our minds in this context is **Wood** itself. It is a very common surname today (there are 185 listed in my local 'phone book). The name has a number of forms, each typical of a certain region: **Weald**, for example, is inclined to be found in the south and south-east of England, while **Wald**, **Walde** and **Wold** are commoner further north in the Anglian counties. There are possibly as many as twenty forms of the word to be found in surnames today. A man may have earned such a name from the place where he lived, or it may have described his work as a **Woodman**, cutting trees for building purposes or for the making of roof tiles, called 'shingles', which were often used for the roofs of the dwellings of the better-off inhabitants. The surname **Shingles** itself exists, though it is quite rare (I note just 1 in my telephone directory, though nearly 200 bearers of the name nationwide) and recalls this specialised craft. **Shingler** too, is a rarity, though the **Spooner** also made wooden tiles as well as spoons.

So general is its meaning that the **Woodman**'s occupation too, may have been of a very general nature, including the clearing of areas of scrub and bushes. The cutting of wood was described in various ways according to its subsequent use or the local vernacular. The following are all found: **Hacker**, **Cleaver**, **Capstick** (that is 'cope stake'), **Cutbush**, **Sawyer** and **Tallboy** (from the French 'taille bois', cut wood). In this context, the axe would seem an obvious tool to give rise to a surname and indeed, the name **Axe** does exist, though it is rare today. Whether the surname derives from the occupational use of the axe or from a mediæval dweller near the Devonshire River **Axe**, may not be possible to determine in most cases.

Another woodland occupation was that of the charcoal burner. This peasant often led a completely solitary life in the woods, making charcoal, called simply 'col' in those times and it is from the charcoal burner's humble task we have inherited the names **Colyer** (which is the original spelling), **Collier** and **Coleman**. By the end of the 1960s, there were estimated to be no more than a dozen skilled charcoal burners left in England and by now there will probably be fewer still, although, in these days of fashionable country crafts, there is a movement to revive such lost occupations. **Cole** was usually a nickname for one with a dark complexion or swarthy skin, though it may have been applied to the charcoal burner, too. The surname **Colman**, however, has a quite different ancestry – it derives from the Old Irish personal name Columban, borne by an Irish missionary and abbot at the end of the 6th century.

Most towns and villages were located close to a stream or a river, over which was the occasional bridge. At the more important bridges, a bridge-keeper was to be seen, collecting tolls from those whose business brought them across the water. However, simply living against the bridge may have been sufficient to acquire the nickname **Bridge**. It is worth noticing, however, that the very similar name **Bridges** usually indicates an ancestor from the Belgian town of Bruges, rather than having a root in the English word bridge.

The man who caught fish, whether from the sea, the rivers or as the lord's appointed fish catcher, easily earned the nickname **Fish** or **Fisher**. Also near the river in many localities, could be found the reed cutter and the surname **Redman** ('reed man') can originate from this man's job, as well as being a nickname for one who had a red face or ginger hair. The **Reeder** may have been the user of reeds, like the **Thatcher** (or **Thacker**) on the roofs of town dwellings.

It was often necessary for the bailiff to keep a man employed laying snares where foxes were known to be found, as these crafty animals were a constant menace to poultry and lambs. In this connection, it would seem that **Trapper** is an obvious source for an occupational surname and I have located a single holder of the name, though **Trapp** is occasionally to be found. This surname was more probably acquired by one whose job was to set traps for other animals than foxes: badgers, rabbits, squirrels and so forth. The fox hunter, however, was known as the **Todhunter** in the north of the kingdom and often as the **Todman** in the south, a 'todde' being the common word for a fox. An interesting, though rather odd name, worth a mention here, is **Wontner**, a catcher of moles or 'wants', as they were sometimes called.

Wild honey was greatly prized by the peasantry, for it was the only sweetener available to them other than the juices of berries and fruits, that were to be gathered only in the autumn and which were smaller and less sweet than we are used to in some of today's scientifically developed fruits. Peasants would take the occasional bee-swarm from its precarious place in the tree and transfer it to a crude wooden hive in the hope that it would remain there and provide them with a slender source of honey for a while. Bees were sometimes kept in hives in the gardens of a manor too, both for their honey for the lord's table and for their wax (for use in ointments, medicines and candles). The bee-keeper's endeavours are remembered in the names **Beeman** and **Waxman**.

Where there was good stone to be found, it was laboriously hewn out of the ground by men with only the simplest of tools. The **Stonehewer**, **Stonier** and **Stanier** were such labourers. Clay pits too, were places of labour, for it was from the **Clayman** that the **Potter**, the **Crocker** and the town brick-maker obtained their raw materials. The surname **Clay** is more often found nowadays than the name **Clayman**, though there is one of each to be found in my current telephone book. One source of the surname **Clare** is the 'clayer' – not the clay digger this time, but the labourer who weatherproofed walls by daubing them with clay (known as wattle-and-daub work), a sort of mediæval plasterer.

In Cornwall there had been extensive mining for tin ore (known as 'tinstone' or 'cassiterite') since pre-Roman times and which still flourished during the mediæval period. It is likely that the surnames **Minor** and **Mines** reflect this work and similar activities in the Midlands and Yorkshire, where it was iron ore that was dug. The value of coal as a fuel was appreciating and was mined in an increasing number of shallow pits in the northern counties of England.

Robin Hood

It seems that those occupations from beyond the village boundary have produced fewer surnames than those from within the village itself. This is largely explained by the fact that there were far fewer peasants who preferred a life away from habitation, which was much less secure than the safety of a small settlement or a town. In some districts there were outlaws living off the land and were always ready to rob travellers of money and peasants of livestock. The most notorious of history's outlaws is of course, Robin Hood and it might be interesting to look briefly at the legend, since it falls within the surname-forming period.

The earliest mention of the name seems to be in a York assize document from the year 1226, which records the seizing of the property and goods of one, 'Robertus Hod, fugitivus' – an outlaw. He seems, at that time, to have inhabited the forests around Barnsdale in Yorkshire, though by the early 15th century, the stories about him had proliferated and moved his territory about a hundred miles southwards to the forests around Nottingham. There are various opinions about his true identity and even whether he existed at all. However, he and his band of men, mythical or not, display an interesting collection of names, which look to us very much like fixed surnames – a result of the 15th and subsequent centuries' embracing of the idea of surnames, no doubt. The name **Hood**, itself, could have referred to the maker of hoods, but it is more likely to have been purely a nickname applied to (or assumed by) one who wore a distinctively shaped or coloured hood. As for the Merrie Men, the ones who come most readily to mind are Little John, Will Scarlet, Much the Miller's Son and Alan Adale. **Little** is quite a common surname and was often a straightforward nickname, describing the diminutive size of an individual. However, if we are at all sympathetic to the legend of Robin Hood and knowing the Englishman's taste for understatement and irony, the nickname may have arisen in may cases because of the unusually *great* height of the man. (I recall that, during my early school years in the 1950s, a large friend of mine was nicknamed 'Tiny'; so the partiality for paradox flourishes, as it always has, even at school!).

The same may be true in the case of **Much** (also sometimes found as **Mutch**). Either he was a large man, as it says, or it is sarcastic and he was diminutive in stature. Will **Scarlett**, as we know him today, may have had strikingly reddish hair, perhaps even a florid complexion or his tunic may simply have been red in colour. It is interesting to notice, however, that in the early ballads about Robin Hood, Will appears with a variety of names: Scarlock, Scatheloke and Scadlock, all of which point to the ginger colour of his hair.

Lastly, the name **Adale**. This name meant 'at the valley' – an example of a local feature being used to identify an individual, though the surname may now have ceased to exist.

Each of the names above, except probably Adale, is to be found as a surname today and one can't help but wonder whether a present day Scarlett or Much might just be the descendant of a merry 13th century forest dweller.

THE CHURCH

There were (and still are) so many officials and churchmen of varying ranks and disciplines, that it will come as no surprise to find that we have acquired many surnames from this great body, sometimes from their titles as clergymen themselves and sometimes through nicknames gained by those laymen who acted the parts in pageants and miracle plays.

There were several branches of the mediæval Church, each having its own body of executive members. To the peasants, however, the Church's most familiar and approachable representative was the **Priest**, who was appointed by the lord of the manor and may have risen from the ranks of the villeins themselves, by displaying more than the common degree of intelligence and interest in the world around him. He would receive his initial, basic training from the existing **Priest**, before his appointment to his own living, part of which was a small property called the 'glebe' or 'gield'. The **Priest** fulfilled so many roles amongst his band of peasants, that their respect for him was probably greater than for any other member of their simple community. As their preacher, teacher, counsellor, comforter and physician, the **Priest** was the one, above all others, in whom the common folk could put their trust.

Possibly the earliest written instance of the designation 'priest', was in the year 963, when one, Aelfsige Preost is recorded.[1] Later, however, the word **Parson** gradually became more common as a title. The surname we meet today is nearly always the possessive form **Parsons**, which referred, not directly to the parson himself, but to one who lived or worked at the parson's house. **Parsonage** too, though much rarer, has the same source. In the same way, **Prescott** (and **Prestcott**) meant 'servant, or dweller at the priest's cottage'. In the mid 13th century the word **Vicar** begins to gain ground and like **Parsons**, we mostly meet it as **Vicars** or **Vickers** – one who lived at, or served at the vicar's dwelling. In spite of pre-Conquest campaigns in favour of celibacy, village priests were quite commonly married and the surnames **Parsons**, **Vicars** and **Vickers** could also refer to 'the child of the parson or vicar'. However, we must not forget that the origins of many surnames lie in the mediæval pageants and the performers in these pageants often played the same role every year, so that it was inevitable that in the minds of the simple folk, the actors became associated with the characters they played, thus earning themselves an obvious nickname.

Whereas the **Priest** was a settled cleric, having his own fixed living, the **Friar** was a roving preacher, travelling on foot from one district to another, teaching those who would listen. Friars, too, were sometimes not as strict in the observance of their vows of celibacy as their order

---

1. G. Tengvik. (1958) *Old English Bynames*. Almquist & Wiksell.

demanded, as Chaucer hints about Hubert the Friar in The Canterbury Tales:

"He kept his tippet *(cape)* stuffed with pins for curls, and pocket knives to give to pretty girls ....."

There is no doubt that many a **Friar** fathered a child or two, who might become known amongst the peasants by his (or her) father's title. The word **Friar** is derived from the Latin 'frater', via the Old French 'frere' and meant 'brother' and may sometimes imply just that, having no connection with the cleric at all. The variations **Fryer, Frere** and **Frear** are occasionally found as surnames too.

There are, however, other explanations for the original acquisition of the nickname as we shall see, in which the **Friar** shares his contribution to posterity not only with the **Monk**, but with the holders of more exalted offices within the Church: the **Prior, Dean, Bishop, Abbot** and even the **Pope**. These names occur too frequently in mediæval times for their meanings to be taken at face value. It is surely unthinkable that the all of the original bearers of the nicknames were the results of illicit unions between such men and peasant girls.

Munn is another form of **Monk**, as is **Moon**, acquired by some close relative to the monk perhaps. A servant at a nearby monastery was likely to have been called **Munns** or **Monkhouse**. The principal of the abbey was the **Abbot**, and his deputy was the **Prior** (seen also today as **Pryor**): important and conspicuous men whose bearing and mannerisms might well have brought forth clever mimicry from a saucy peasant, who thus earned for himself a clerical nickname. Most of the high ranking clergy would have had lay relatives, some of whom, no doubt, would have been pleased to have been associated with the title of their distinguished kinsman. The same must be true of the name **Bishop**, although the ceremony of the 'boy bishop', begun in York in 1221, must often have led to the retention of the nickname by the boys thus honoured.

The nicknaming process was clearly at work when we come to consider how a man might have acquired the name **Pope** (**Pape** is a later variation). This nickname may have been jokingly applied to more than one village priest by jesting peasants, but it must also have arisen, like so many others in this Church group, from the roles played (often by the same man each time) in pageants and plays. It is interesting, in passing, to notice that the only Englishman ever to have been elected Pope, took his office at this time. He was Nicholas **Breakspear**, who assumed the title Pope Adrian IV in 1154, though his short tenure as pontiff (only 5 years) is unlikely to have given much impetus to the popularising of either the name **Adrian** or **Pope**.

Canon (and possibly **Cannon**) may have recalled one who lived, served or studied at the residence of this cathedral dignitary, while

Deacon and **Deakin** allude to the priest's official who attended to the more worldly affairs of the Church.

The surname **Dean** probably only rarely referred in any way to the churchman, since most records of the early occurrence of the name include either 'de' (meaning *of*) or 'atte' (*at the*), as in Ralph de Dene (1066)[1] and William atte Dene (1296)[2], suggesting one who lived in a dell or hollow, or came from one of the many villages of this name. It is only when we encounter **Deans**, with its genitive 's', that we may be faced with a descendant or servant of the cleric.

In an almost wholly male-orientated society such as existed In the middle ages, it will be entirely understandable that there will not be many surnames that have come from women's occupations or their domestic situations. We have already noticed that there is an occasional feminine form of some names, indicated by simply incorporating an 's' or an 'x' into the masculine word: **Webber/Webster**, **Baker/Baxter**, **Brewer/Brewster** and **Dyer/Dexter** are some we have met. Female clergy were less numerous and less significant than their male counterparts in the overall scheme of monasticism and consequently, we cannot be surprised that are very few surnames which derive directly from female clergy. The obvious one is **Nunn**, a name applied either to one who had been a nun or whose close relative (sister perhaps) had become a nun, or even as an unflattering nickname given to a man whose mannerisms somehow reminded his fellows of those of a nun. **Nunns**, like **Monks**, was probably genitive and indicative of one who served or worked at the nunnery.

A fairly common name today is **Church** and we must assume that it was given to one who lived next to, served in, or had some special connection with the church building or service. The same may be true of **Chapel** (and **Chapple**), though this surname may equally derive from the chamberlain's official who was in charge of the lord's personal chapel (see the section *In the Hall - the Household*).

During the surname-forming period of English history, the Crusading fervour reached its zenith and many men were periodically returning from the Holy Land after long campaigns of noble purpose. Non-combatant pilgrims too, made hazardous ventures towards Palestine. Those who returned safely frequently bore treasured souvenirs of their adventure, often in the form of palm leaves and thus the nickname **Palmer** arose. In the words of the 16th century scholar, William Camden:

"Some (men) from that which they commonly carryed, as **Palmer**, in regard that Pilgrims carried Palme when they returned from Hierusalem"[3].

---

1. P. H. Reaney (1976) A Dictionary of British Surnames. Routledge & Keegan Paul.
2. Ibid.
3. William Camden (1586). Remains Concerning Britain (1607 edition).

Thus, we have inherited an interesting variety of surnames from the mediæval Church, most of which are true nicknames, but also there is a scattering of occupational names, together with one or two that originate from the church building itself, a local feature. Many of the names I have mentioned here have more variations of spelling than is convenient to list and there are several other rare names I haven't mentioned, which have rather more obscure ecclesiastical connections. However, the two dozen or so surnames listed here form the common body of our surnames whose origins lie in the mediæval Church and its functionaries.

THE LORD'S HOUSEHOLD

As soon as William Of Normandy had declared himself King of England (he was crowned on Christmas Day, 1066), he set about the task of crushing all opposition within the realm and confiscating the lands of the native English barons. This was no easy undertaking, even for such an unrelentingly ruthless autocrat as William. As we know, it was not until the year 1085, when England was again under foreign threat (this time from Denmark), that the King felt a pressing need for a thorough fiscal and military appraisal of his kingdom. At Christmas 1085, William directed that an immediate national survey be carried out, resulting in the Domesday Book.

King William had first divided his realm into three parts: one quarter of the whole he retained as his own personal domain, a second quarter was made over to the tenancy of the Church and the remaining half he apportioned in grants, called 'fiefs' or 'feuds', to his faithful Norman supporters. Thus the King retained sole ownership of the whole of England, while the Church and his noble adherents gained valuable royal patronage. In return for these rewards, his great secular tenants were required to give counsel and provide military service in the form of a specified number of armed knights, who were always available to the King.

The King's most powerful Tenants-in-Chief are thought to have numbered about 170, each holding estates of varying size and number, according to his status. Each estate was divided into manageable districts called 'manors', the greatest tenants numbering several hundred manors in their tenure. At the other end of the scale, there were many tenants whose holdings amounted to no more than perhaps twenty manors and who were themselves, sub-tenants of greater barons.

So we see that there was a fairly straightforward basic framework:

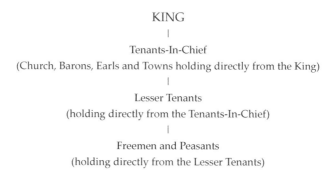

Although this concept looks uncomplicated, more intricate sub-structures soon evolved within its fabric: villages divided between two manors or villeins owing allegiance to two lords, for example.

It was long believed that, to ensure loyalty and to prevent a baron easily raising an army for his own ends, the King had arranged that the estates of each Tenant were well dispersed across the kingdom. However, this belief has been shown to be untenable and is without documentary support[1]. Nevertheless, the distribution of the estates compelled the Tenants to travel between their possessions, inspecting their lands, holding courts to settle disputes, hearing pleas and dispensing justice, to say nothing of their much enjoyed hunting in the forests. The more powerful Barons built themselves mighty castles. Indeed we learn from Domesday (1086-87) that in the twenty years previously, 49 castles had been built. There were another 40 in existence by the end of the century.

Most manors, however, were controlled from the 'Hall', which in many cases, was nothing more grand than a well-timbered house, but could also be a stone and wood structure on a more extensive scale, which would require a staff of servants of various ranks and skills to maintain it and to supervise the running of the manorial lands.

In the Hall – the Household

The lord's house manager, who lived at the Hall, came to be known as the **Steward** (from the Old English 'sty', a house, and 'weard', guard or watchman) and more commonly seen today as **Stewart** in England and **Stuart** in Scotland. The steward's principal responsibility was to ensure the smooth and effective running of the household, which entailed organising the servants, maintaining provisions and dealing with the

---

1. W. Stubbs (1903) Constitutional History of England. Clarendon Press.

inevitable petty arguments, bickerings and quarrels that will always arise within a body of servants. The common surname **Hall** may also have been used to refer to the **Steward** at this time, since he was based at the Hall, or the villagers may have applied the nickname to one of their number who worked there, but lived in the village. The less common surname **House** probably arose in the same ways.

When there was news at the hall of the forthcoming arrival of the Baron or Earl, there would be great activity of preparation. The grandee would arrive, accompanied by his personal retinue of servants and officials, the number varying according to their master's status. The lord's **Chamberlain** (often shortened to **Chambers** or **Chalmers**) attended his master in his private chamber, kept his wardrobe and looked after his personal effects and money. However, as the 14th century progressed, the office of **Chamberlain** became somehow rather devalued and the title would be increasingly applied to one in attendance at inns and hostelries, so that the modern bearer of this surname may not necessarily descend from the important household official of a high-ranking nobleman.

Another senior house official was the **Chancellor**. He was nobleman's secretary and keeper of the official records who, assisted by his staff of **Clerk**s (nowadays usually seen as **Clark** and **Clarke**), was also responsible for care of the chapel. The **Chancellor** may well have invested another individual with special responsibility for the chapel, in which case the nickname **Chapel** would arise.

Two very junior members of the personal household staff of the lord were the **Page** and the **Squire**. Wealthier parents would usually wish their sons to be trained for knighthood, a process that could only be done under the guidance and tutelage of a nobleman. With the lord's permission, the child would be brought to the hall or castle at the age of seven or eight and would begin his training by attending the lady as her **Page**, taking his lessons with her own children, while all the time learning about the affairs of the household. Later on, he would be taught how to wait at his master's table and would be given small errands to run. Later still, perhaps at about the age of fourteen, the **Page** would ascend to the position of **Squire**, of whom there were usually several per household. Now his duties included carving at table for his master, keeping the lord's armour bright and assisting his master at tournaments, while learning the arts of war from older squires and knights.

Every **Squire** would look forward, with impatience no doubt, to the day when he himself would become a **Knight**. If he had fulfilled his apprenticeship to his master's satisfaction, the ceremony of knighthood would take place when the **Squire** reached the age of twenty-one. However, automatic elevation to knighthood was not assured and not every squire's performance met with the lord's approval, leaving some unknighted, which may partly account for the rise of the surnames **Page** and **Squire**.

During the 11th century, the **Knight** was hardly more than a professional soldier in the household of a Baron and was usually referred to as a 'housecarl'. By the middle of the 12th century, however, the knight's status had increased and he was now expected to own his armour and horses and to maintain his own household with his own servants, pages and squires. As a landholder, he would find himself the lord of perhaps a dozen or so villages, with all the feudal responsibilities this position entailed. The **Knight** was pledged to give forty days a year military service to his lord and serve him as a mounted soldier for at least two months in times of war, all at his own expense.

At meal times and especially at feasts, wine was served at the lord's table by the **Butler** (originally from the Old French word 'bouteiller', a bottler in charge of the cellar). The **Butler** too, was in charge of the wines and later, the general pantry, and would have worked closely with the **Spencer** (and **Spenser**), who dispensed provisions from the **Spence** (that is, the larder). These two surnames clearly recall the servant in charge of issuing provisions to the kitchen.

In charge of the kitchen itself, was the **Cook**, who doubtless exercised a ruthless authority over the kitchen hands (or **Kitchener**s). As the lord and his guests ate, his **Napier** would be at hand with a supply of clean napkins – a necessary accessory, since fingers were the main eating implements – while another servant may well have been close by to offer a small basin, or 'laver' (Latin 'lavare', to wash) of clean water, in which the diners could wash their fingers. Such a servant would naturally have acquired the nickname **Laver**, as a consequence.

A surname coming from the same Latin root as **Laver** is **Lavender**, which would later be shortened to **Launder** and even **Lander**. The task of the **Lavender**s, who were usually women, was the washing of clothes in the laundry house.

Messages between manors, or from one Baron to another, were carried by a trained **Messenger** on a good horse. The **Messenger** readily gained a variety of nicknames in different localities. Among many such names to have become surnames in their own right, are the following: **Lightfoot**, **Race**, **Startup**, **Treadwell**, **Treadaway**, **Gellatly** (that is, 'go lightly'), **Fleet** and even **Foot** itself. These are clearly true nicknames in the sense we understand the term today.

Security inside the Hall or castle was preserved by the house soldiers called **Ward**s, a word which has come down to us almost unmodified from the Old English 'weard', a watchman or sentry. From this ancient word comes our modern word guard, though **Garde**, as a surname, can be found in a document of 1275, where one, John le Garde, is mentioned[1].

---

1. P. H. Reaney (1976) A Dictionary of British Surnames. Routledge & Keegan Paul.

In the lord's stables

In and around the stables there were to be found a number of servants whose designated tasks have provided us with some interesting surnames. Very early on, that is in the late 11th and early 12th centuries, the most important domestic officer was the 'comes stabuli', the 'count of the stable'. In everyday speech, these two Latin words soon became compressed into a single word, **Constable**. This official was in overall charge of the daily running of the noble stables. However, this use of the word gradually disappeared and it came to signify a chief officer in the household. Next in importance to the **Constable** would have been the **Marshall**, whose responsibilities were the horses, dogs and hawks. Indeed, this word has risen to impressive heights in more recent times and we tend to forget that the original holder of the title was little more than a stable lad! **Maskell** and **Mascall** are variations of the surname.

At the stable we will also find servants with different responsibilities for different kinds of horse: the **Steadman** ('steed man') attended the great war horses and the mounts of the fighting knights; the **Palfreyman** looked after the smaller pack-carrying horses (the 'palfreys'), while the **Runciman** had charge of the nags (the 'rouncies'), which were the general riding animals.

The important craft of the **Sadler** required the making and repairing of the horse gear, saddles and harness. The surnames **Seller** and **Cellier** (words derived from the French word 'selle', a saddle) meant the same as **Sadler**, though to complicate matters, **Seller** often meant what it says – a seller of goods – and so it is almost impossible to know from which occupation the name has sprung.

Finally, a word which has strong associations today with the care of horses, **Groom**, signified at the time no more than a general servant.

The lands around the Hall

Within the extensive grounds surrounding the great halls of mediæval England were employed a number of workers with distinct duties. Firstly, the gardeners, a very general term, which included men having specified tasks which have given rise to the surnames **Plant**, **Mower**, **Weed** and of course, to **Gardener**, itself. The **Parker** did his best to keep the impudent opportunists of the local peasantry out of the lord's private lands for, if a deer were taken and killed, the culprit, if caught, could expect little mercy: mutilation or execution were commonly administered. In the year 1217, however, under pressure from the great barons, the ten-year-old King Henry III lightened the harshness of the forest laws. Even so, trespass and the taking of venison remained a severely punishable crime and the **Forester** was a well-trained and resolute servant of his lord.

The forests were maintained as the exclusive retreats of the King and his great barons and hunting was always a favourite recreation, which these men relished. Skilled and experienced men were employed to enable them to pursue their sports with both enjoyment and success. Such a man was the **Falconer**, whose name is most often seen today as **Faulkner**. His principal undertaking was the care and training of the lord's hunting falcons, which were likely to have been an expensive investment for his master. The highest ranking barons were permitted to acquire the female peregrine, which was preferred to the smaller and less aggressive male bird. Nobles of lower status had to be content with goshawks and even sparrowhawks. Mention of this last species reminds us that a fairly familiar modern surname is **Hawk**, no doubt an alternative nickname for the **Falconer** in many cases, though it must also have been given to one having distinctly hawk-like features, such as a small, curved, sharp nose or bird-like eyes. A name still more suggestive of the falconer's skill is **Hawker**, especially when we find mention of one, Robert le Haukere, in a Gloucestershire document of 1214[1].

It was the custom of Norman kings and other great noblemen to retain professional huntsmen to kill deer for the castle larders and this occupation must be one source of the surnames **Hunt** and **Hunter**. It would be a mistake, however, to assume that these names were solely acquired by hunters of royal or noble appointment: many an audacious poacher from the peasant classes might be nicknamed 'the hunter' (out of earshot of the **Bailiff**, the **Parker** or the **Granger** of course). The same may be said of the **Fowler**, a taker of fowls, or one who prepared them for the lord's table.

Assisting the **Forester** (**Forster, Forrester** and **Foster** are familiar alternatives today) in the management of the lord's woods and plantations in many districts, was the **Woodward**, who was often an elected holder of this office, in much the same way as was the **Reeve**.

Having now discovered a number of surnames deriving from the worldly pleasures of the high-born, we might wonder what names we have inherited from the more spiritual side of noble life, particularly since the notions of Heaven and especially Hell, exercised a powerful influence on the mediæval minds of both high-born and low-born.

It may seem surprising that there was really only one cleric who attended to the lord's spiritual needs and from whose office we have inherited a surname. He was the **Chaplain** (also appearing as **Chaplin** and occasionally, **Caplin** today). In some households he may have had an assistant called the 'clerk of the chapel', whose duties included the supervision of the vestments and silver, leaving the **Chaplain** free to perform the mass when called upon, as his lord travelled between

---

1. P. H. Reaney (1976) A Dictionary of British Surnames. Routledge & Keegan Paul.

his manors. The **Chaplain** was, however, but a step above the general domestic servants of the household, in spite of his title.

The Fighting Men

If we now turn to the military side of the mediæval picture, we shall find a crop of names arising from the soldiers of different categories, whose special skills were essential in times of battle. As I mentioned earlier, the **Knight** soon became an important figure in the baron's contribution to the king's fighting forces and, mounted on his great warhorse and clad in polished armour, he would have been an impressive and menacing sight as he rode across the battlefield.

The footsoldiers, on the other hand, were regarded by the early Norman professional fighters as rather contemptible, unskilled lackeys, but, as time went on, the **Bowman** and **Archer** became vital to the success of any campaign, so much so, that in 1363, King Edward the III enacted that every Sunday and feast day all London men between the ages of sixteen and sixty must attend the butts for archery practice.

Before the introduction of the longbow, which came into extensive use in the 13th century, the Normans employed the shorter crossbow. This weapon was fixed to a wooden stock and its drawstring had to be levered into the firing position before a wooden bolt could be discharged by releasing a trigger. The French name for this weapon was 'arablast' and its operator has given us the surname **Arblaster**. The crossbow, however, had two serious performance weaknesses when set against the longbow. The obvious shortcoming was that in the time it took to load and fire a single bolt, even by an expert arblaster, an experienced longbowman would have accurately discharged up to half a dozen arrows into the ranks of the enemy. The crossbow's second failing was that it did not possess the reach or penetrative power of the new longbow. Evidence of the effectiveness of the latter is seen in the triumphs of the English over the French, at the battles of Crécy (1346), Poitiers (1356) and Agincourt (1415), in each of which the French forces outnumbered the Englishmen by significant margins.

Two artisans usually overlooked in the preparation of the weapons were the **Stringer**, who prepared the gut and strung the bows and the bow maker himself, the **Bowyer.**

Such names as **Spears**, **Shakespeare** and **Shakeshaft** remind us that, though the mounted knight may have gained the military homage in later years, there were other important elements in the battle forma-tions – the spearmen. These infantrymen took up their positions behind the lines of **Archers** and could make a considerable contribution to the outcome. The king and his barons rallied their fighting men around their personal, distinctively decorated standards, held aloft by their bearers, who are remembered today (though more often in Scotland) in the surname **Bannerman**.

The surname **Gunn**, of which there are 20 entries in my local telephone book, looks a promising candidate for inclusion in this section. However, its probable origin lies either in the Norse word for a battle, 'gunnr', or else in the Norse woman's name Gunnar, rather than in the Middle English word 'gonner', a term later applier to the soldier in charge of the cannon and gunpowder. Since the earliest known English use of guns in battle was in the siege of Calais by the army of King Edward III in 1346, it places the name a little late in the surname forming period. But still, the firing of such a novelty might still educe a nickname, even at a relatively late stage. Dr Reaney[1] notes one, Thomas le gonner, in the year 1285, which may clinch its origin.

The same may well apply to the surname **Gunner** (only 1 in my telephone book) – Norse in origin rather than English.

Entertainments

Our final look at life in and around the early mediæval English village and Hall concerns those whose talents lay in the entertainment of others, peasant and noble alike. There are not many in this group, but their legacy in our surnames is an agreeably welcome one.

When receiving a visiting nobleman, the local lord would almost certainly require music and singers, together with jugglers and acrobats, to entertain and amuse the company after the feasting. A high-ranking or wealthy nobleman would have been able to retain his own troupes of performers and it is from these that we have gained an important set of artistic surnames. The favourite instrument was a small, plucked harp, perhaps because of its Biblical associations and the **Harper** was a most respected performer, if we are to set any store by the reward of a grant of land made by the Earl of Gloucester to his own **Harper** in 1183. The **Harper** was usually an accomplished **Singer** too, whose repertoire was wide in both theme and sentiment and who must have been welcome in any company. Another harp-like instrument was the psaltery, which may be a source of the surname **Salter**, though a more likely origin of this name is one who sold salt for the preservation of meats and fish.

Whistles and pipes of various sorts were common instruments too and **Whistler** and **Piper** were obvious nicknames given to the players. However, the Englishmen's pronunciation of the French word 'oiseleur' (a bird-catcher) is another source of the surname **Whistler**.

Several violin-like instruments were also in common use: the fiddle

---

1.   P. H. Reaney (1976) A Dictionary of British Surnames. Routledge & Keegan Paul.

(called a vielle), the crowd (from the Welsh 'crwth') and the rote (or rotte) were the three bowed instruments most likely to be heard and it is from the performers on these that we have obtained the surnames **Fiddler**, **Viddler**, **Crowder**, **Crowther**, and **Rutter**.

Of the plucked instruments to be heard, apart from the harp and psaltery, already mentioned, there was the lute, the instrument perhaps most associated in our minds with the mediæval period and due in no small measure no doubt, to the fanciful whims of 20th century film makers. Its player was the **Luter**, a name transformed into an alternative, **Luther**. Surprisingly, the surname **Lutman**, which also looks as though it belongs here, is a corruption of 'little-man'.

Dancing was a popular pastime in both village and court and the surname **Dance** recalls the paid leader of the court dancers, while **Hopper** was a nickname given to a particularly spirited performer, whose leaping actions were loudly applauded. The dancers were frequently accompanied by the beating of a small drum, called a **Tabor**, the blowing of a **Horn** (by the **Hornblower**) and sometimes, by the sounds of a keyless trumpet played by the **Trumper**.

Unfortunately, acrobats and jugglers have left us with very few names. Current nationwide electoral rolls list 29 instances of **Juggler** itself, indicating that it is clinging to existence, but with only a single instance of **Tumbler** in the London telephone directory and 8 others recorded in electoral registers, this name may be heading for extinction. **Tumber**, however, crops up rather more often, but this name may refer to an acrobatic dancer.

THE TOWN

Before the Norman Conquest, English towns had tended to grow up either near rivers, especially at ancient crossing places where the water was shallow, or where important overland routes met. Sometimes settlements arose at sheltered coastal locations too, where the sea would provide some of the villagers' food. Wherever the community established itself, there would develop a small centre of exchange where both craftsmen and the unskilled could sell their wares or their labour. These boroughs eventually enjoyed the protection of the king, who would levy various dues from the merchandise and markets. After the Conquest, little changed for some time, except that some of the greater feudal tenants began to establish towns or boroughs on their own estates by petitioning the king for the right to hold a weekly market at a convenient place such as at a crossroads. Once permission had been granted, the settlement might grow, either of its own accord, or else by a certain amount of planning imposed by the lord. However, the granting of a royal charter was no guarantee that the newly established community would flourish: about half of such attempts failed to develop the characteristics of a thriving market town.

By modern standards, a mediæval town would be no more than a large village and a settlement of six thousand inhabitants would be considered important. Such a place was Oxford, which, by the time of the Domesday survey in 1086, was large enough to be called a city:

> "... adjuncto molinoque infra *civitate* habebat." (*"... as well as the mill he had within the city"*)

However, a few lines later, the scribe seems unsure, for he now writes:

> " In ipsa *villa* ...." (*"In this town ....."*)

Oxford was granted a charter of liberties and rights by King Henry II in 1147 and a further grant (with seal) was made in 1191 by King Richard I ('the Lionheart'), each endorsing the foundation of a public market on Wednesdays, in an area around the main crossroads known as Carfax. A later charter (1301) permitted a second market to be held on Saturdays.

In some respects, Oxford's fortunes were to be exceptional for, as the University grew, the antagonisms between students and townsfolk increased. Quarrels were frequent and sometimes led to bloodshed, as on St Scholastica's Day (10th February) in 1355, when more than seventy people were killed in a fierce riot. Few towns suffered this level of disorder, but all towns must have had their own problems from time to time, with disputes arising between tradesmen, craftsmen and civic authorities. It is to these citizens that we now must turn to discover a huge variety of names which have come down through the centuries to us.

The Workers in Metal

The village smiths had to be general workers of iron, competently making simple tools and utensils, shoeing a horse and mending a bucket. The town smiths, on the other hand, were often specialists: the **Lockier** (seen also as **Lokyer** and **Lock** today) made locks and keys, the **Cutler** (sometimes **Coulter**, **Coulthard** and very rarely now, **Cutner**) made knives. The variation **Coulter** illustrates a curious, but characteristic phenomenon in the spoken English of the middle ages and later: this is the exchanging of position of two consecutive letters within a word, the effect of which seems either to smooth out a small jerk or unevenness in the pronunciation or, as in this example, to give a slightly sharper emphasis to each syllable. The same exchange has happened in the surnames **Cripps (Crisp)**, **Sansom (Samson)** and **Thropp (Thorp)** among others.

Another knife-maker was the **Naismith**, whom we have already met in the village and who probably made iron nails too, a commodity also turned out by the **Naylor**. Scythes were the speciality of the **Sixsmith**.

As I mentioned in the section, 'Work in the village', there became so many different types of **Smith** within the towns and cities, that it is hardly surprising that **Smith** has long been the most common English surname. The suffix '-smith' has also formed an important group of compounds, thus contributing further to the frequency of the name. The prefix always occurred in one of two forms: either a colour or else the name of the item being made. Colour prefixes are to be seen in **Blacksmith** (a general iron-master), **Brownsmith** (a specialist in copper work), **Greensmith** (a maker of brass articles), **Greysmith** (a lead worker) and **Whitesmith** (a tin specialist). The apron, tools, bench and crucibles of the **Whitesmith** must have had a perpetual white coating of tin oxide, which probably accounts for the nickname. The **Brownsmith** and the **Whitesmith** also produced the alloy bronze by melting together tin and copper. The surname **Whitesmith** is rare today: there are only four entries in the London telephone directory.

To these colour surnames can be added three more, though they are not strictly colours: the **Goldsmith** and **Silversmith** produced the metals for coinage, jewellery and decorative inlays, as well as plate and vessels for both ceremonial use and for the tables of the wealthy classes, while the **Coppersmith** worked the soft red metal into strikingly polished ornaments and decorations and the occasional piece of bronzeware. **Goldsmith** is the only one of this group which occurs with any frequency today (212 in the London telephone directory), the rest having receded into the distance and may be on the way to following into extinction such interesting names as Comsmyth ('comb smith', still current in 1590)[1], Blaydesyith ('blade smith')[2], Bokelsmyth ('buckle smith')[3] and Ankersmyth ('anchor smith')[4], amongst others.

Lead ore (galena) was mined in only a few places and was expensive. The metal's principal applications were in the roofing of churches and other important buildings and in leaded windows that were beginning to make their appearance at this time. It was soft and therefore an easy

---

1. H. Reaney (1979 edition) The Origin of English Surnames Routledge & Keegan Paul.

2. Ibid.

3. Ibid.

4. Ibid.

metal to work. Its Latin name of 'plumbum' has given rise to the names **Plummer** and the much rarer surnames **Plumber** and **Plumb**.

Although the **Greensmith** has been mentioned already as a specialist in brass work, another artisan, the **Brazier** (often transformed into **Brasher** and **Braisher**) also practised his skills upon this alloy that, in the form of engraved sheets, began to supplant stone memorials in churches from early in the 13th century.

It has been estimated both from preserved examples of mediæval coins and from those recovered by archæologists, that, in the year of the Conquest (1066), there were seventy official mints throughout England. The king himself, issued licences to moneyers and clearly the surnames **Minter**, **Coyne** and **Money** recall their occupations. It is interesting to note the severe punishment administered by order of King Henry I in 1125, to 94 of the 97 Winchester moneyers, for the crime of flooding the land with 'false money'. They each suffered loss of a hand, as specified by the law. A man's generosity or wealth, may have earned him **Money** as his nickname, as may his miserliness, knowing the Englishman's taste for irony!

The requirement for the finest armour was not great, but all men of noble rank would wish for impressive sets, which took some time and considerable skill in the making. The craftsman here was no ordinary smith, but the armourer. His craft has provided us with the surname **Armer**, while his fellow worker, the master polisher of the finished pieces was the **Frobisher** (or **Furber** for short). Both names derive from imported Norman French words. The fighting noblemen would also wish to specify a sword of the highest affordable quality from the **Blader** (who must also have been known by the friendly nickname **Blades**) and which incorporated an impressive hilt from the hiltsmith (Hildsmith[1] is a lost surname, unfortunately).

Most master craftsmen kept at least one apprentice, who toiled for several years (usually between three and seven years, depending on the guild rules) to acquire his master's expertise. If the guildmaster was satisfied with his work, the apprentice would be elevated to the position of 'journeyman' and would then earn a daily wage (French, 'jour', a day). Some, however, never achieved this transition and may have been nicknamed **Prentice** or **Prentiss** as a consequence, though the name must also have been applied to almost any youth by his family and neighbours on taking up his new place under a master's supervision.

Having considered so many of the metal-smiths, whose trade was vitally important to the commercial well-being of the town, we can now leave them and pass on to a group of individuals whose trades were very different from those of the smiths, but who have left us with an equally

---

1. H. Reaney (1979 edition) The Origin of English Surnames Routledge & Keegan Paul.

interesting set of surnames.

Producers of Animal Goods

The trade centred on leather was of great importance and it has furnished us with a surprising number of surnames. Apart from the **Tanner**, **Barker** and **Botler**, already mentioned in the section 'Work in the Village', there was the **Skinner**, who provided the furs for the trimming and lining of clothes, the skins, usually from the pig and goat, for the making of parchment and hides for the **Shoemaker** (the **Shoesmith**, too) and the **Bolger** (Old French, 'boulgier') who made leather bags, pouches and the like. The **Glover** would require special soft skins for his work and these pelts would come from the **Coney**, a term meaning 'rabbit' and applied to the catcher of these animals. The **Sadler**, who, in some places was called the **Lorrimer**, obtained his hides from the general leather supplier, **Leather** himself. Other related names are **Cheverell**, a specialist in kid leather goods and **Whittier**, meaning 'white leather'. The surnames **Boot** and **Belt** tell their own story of footwear and girdles.

Animals were the source of very many useful products other than leather and we must look at these next. Probably the most familiar name to us in this respect will be **Butcher**. He was, of course, mainly interested in obtaining the meat from carcasses and in the north of England was called the **Bowker**. In Scotland, however, he is still often referred to as the 'flesher', which is one source of the surname **Fletcher**. The other origin of this surname is the French word 'flechier', a maker and seller of arrows. If your name happens to be **Fletcher** therefore, we can only guess at the trade of your ancestor – meat or arrows! However, there were probably more fleshers than fletchers.

Having stripped away the hide and removed the innards and meat from the carcass, what is left that is useful? The answer is – a great deal. The horns, if there were any, were saved for making ornaments, vessels for holding powders and liquids, bugles to be blown and finally, they could be ground into medicinal powders. The individual who did such work was clearly the **Horner**. The hair was shaved off the hide and used by the **Croucher** (now found as **Crouch** too) for stuffing cushions, pillows and mattresses as a cheaper substitute for feathers, which gave a softer filling.

Much of the fat of the carcass was cut away and sold to the **Chandler** and the **Soper**. The first of these made candles from the fat, called 'tallow'. There is a single entry of **Tallow** in the London telephone book and 27 others in electoral registers, indicating that this historic surname survives, but only just. The **Soper** was a soap maker. He boiled the rendered fat with wood ash, a process which would have produced very

disagreeable odours and he must have been unpopular with his neighbours. The candle makers had their own street in London (**Chandler**
Street), close to the Tower, where they would have turned out thousands
of 'tallow dips' every week, by carefully melting the fat and inserting a
wick of flax or rush. This operation from so many workshops must have
filled the neighbourhood air with a perpetual rank and obnoxious odour.
(The best and most expensive candles, however, were those made from
beeswax and gave a clear, bright light). The animal fat could also be made
to yield a thick oil, which would soon become rancid if kept unused and,
like tallow, it could be burned through a wick, though it would produce
only a feeble light while giving off an unwholesome smoke. The 'oil man'
has come down to us as **Ulman**, which occurs in several variations of
spelling, including **Elman**.

Food

Not many names have survived whose origins lie in the names of meats.
Bacon may well have been the nickname given to the man who cured
and sold the flesh of the pig, but it may also have its root in the Old
German personal name Bacus. **Veale** though, probably *was* the nickname
for one who sold calf meat in the town. In this case, though, there are
confusions with **Vale**, a dweller in a valley, as well as with the Old French
'vieil', meaning 'old'. As for **Mutton** and **Lamb**, these names were likely
to have referred both to the **Shepherd** and to the lamb herder. Indeed,
Lamb is still used as a name of affection, especially towards a child and
so it must also have been applied long ago to one with a gentle and
trusting temperament.

The best practical means of preserving meat for the winter months
was by either salting it down (with salt from the **Salter** or **Sauter** and
even **Salt**) or, if there was no salt to be had, by hanging the sides of beef
or mutton in the rafters over the fire so that the smoke kept away the flies
and the flesh was slowly cured. We must wonder at the wholesomeness
of the food of our mediæval forebears, not least from the point of view of
hygiene and, considering the conditions inside the poorer dwellings, of
which there were many in most towns and especially the filth which was
allowed to accumulate in the streets, we shall hardly be surprised at the
frequent outbreaks of food poisoning, amongst many other curses, due
to the imperfect curing of meat. From our standpoint in the 21st century,
it is hardly possible to envisage the everyday conditions that prevailed
in most towns in mediæval times. Town authorities seemed powerless
to enforce repeated instructions to slaughterers not to kill animals in the
streets, nor to dispose of offal and carcasses in the gutters, which were
nothing more than stinking sewers in many places, running with cattle

blood and discarded rotting matter much of the time. The sickening stench was a feature of town life to which the citizens seemed resigned, despite the many attempts to change these nauseating practices. If this were not enough to send us, as time travellers, dashing for our time machine and gasping for clean air, there were the additional contributions made by the fishmongers, the leather tanners and the brick burners, while cats, dogs and rats scratched and rooted amongst the fly-ridden garbage. Yet nearby, we would find the bakers baking bread in the ovens behind their shops in much the same way as they do today. These ovens were said to be 'in the backhouse', which has left us with the unusual surname **Bacchus**, from one who worked in the baker's backhouse. This name looks as though it might have referred to one who loved his ale or wine, after the Greek god Bacchus (also known as Dionysus), but there is probably no connection other than the unexpected spelling.

There were several grades of bread: the best was baked from white wheat-flour and was beyond the means of the labouring class. This 'wastel' bread has given us the surname **Whitbread** (that is 'white bread'), after the baker from whom it could be bought. He would also produce 'cocket' loaves, which were sometimes baked from the finest white flour, but often were of the less well milled product. The commonest bread and the staple of the majority of the citizens, was made from the whole wheat or from unbolted flour (called 'treet') and was very coarse. Unscrupulous bakers had evolved many tricks for swindling their customers. One dodge was to separate a quantity of the customer's flour by cunning sleight of hand, and to substitute an amount of chalk to make up the weight – a punishable offence if proven. Sweet biscuits, called 'simnels' and dainty flat cakes, each out of reach of the poorer folk's purses, might also be made by the baker, who must have earned himself the rather pleasing nickname of **Cakebread** in some places, as a result. In some towns the dough-kneader would often be a woman who was called a 'daye' (Old English 'dæge') and this is one source of the surname **Day**. It is a little surprising that the word 'bread' specifically from the baking trade seems not to have survived as a surname (**Bread** – a very rare surname now – there are none in the London telephone directory and only 8 in electoral registers – probably derives from a rendering of **Braid**, a plaiter of wool).

This may be a good place to discuss the surname **Pye**, which I first mentioned in Chapter One in the section 'The different classes of surname', as it certainly was sometimes a nickname for a maker or seller of pies, as we see in the person of Peter Piebakere (1320)[1]. However, it was also a witty nickname for one who was artful and perhaps just a little light-fingered on occasion, pilfering objects like a magpie. Was William

---

1. P. H. Reaney (1976) A Dictionary of British Surnames. Routledge & Keegan Paul.

le Pye, recorded in a 1296 document[1], one of this type, I wonder? The magpie appeared on tavern signs too, so that a man who lived or worked at such a place might well have found himself called after the bird, as must have been the case with Stephen atte Pye[2] who appears in a London document dated 1347. The surname certainly has colourful possibilities.

From the usual open-fronted shops (still occasionally seen today), fish were laid out for sale by one, inevitably nicknamed **Fish** (the **Fisher** being the fish catcher, as its '-er' suffix would suggest). Weirs had been introduced into many of the country's rivers during this period, in order to limit the movement of fish so that dace, chub, perch, mullet, pike, eels and even the humble minnow were easily taken by the lord's appointed **Fisher**. Such a convenient source of fish was of course a gift to the clandestine poachers who worked the rivers, streams, ponds and marshes. Villages which had a significant fishery were expected to render a proportion of their catches to the lord, while settlements near the coast had the benefit of fish caught offshore, though a render was still due to the lord and catchers of such sea fish were likely to be called after the fish they most often brought ashore: **Haddock** and **Herring** are two such names.

One treat much enjoyed by the mediæval citizen was the flesh of birds. Many a household had its handful of scraggy chickens that scratched around the yards and doorsteps and wandered up and down, providing an occasional egg to supplement the otherwise plain diet. Wild birds, of course, were to be found in great numbers in the woodlands and cleared ground that surrounded the towns and **Fowler** was a well-earned nickname, no doubt. The results of this man's efforts were to be found on many a market stall. The familiar nursery rhyme about the 'four-and-twenty blackbirds baked in a pie', reminds us that any bird that could be caught was eaten: lark, pigeon, thrush, duck, as well as what we now call 'game birds': pheasant, partridge, woodcock, quail and so on. If **Fowler** was the native English word for the bird-catcher, then **Osler** was one rendering of the French word for a bird – 'oiseleur' (another version was **Whistler**). The name **Poulter** also derives from the Norma-French 'pouletier', meaning a poultry seller.

Passing along the town street, we might perceive by its character-istic fragrance, the shop of the **Spicer**. This merchant was assured of a steady and profitable trade in most towns, for spices from the East were in constant demand in order to improve, and often disguise, the flavour of long stored meats in broths and stews. His wares could command high prices, so that only the servants of the better off citizens could afford to visit his shop, unless he also sold the more familiar herbs: fennel, sage,

---

1. P. H. Reaney (1976) A Dictionary of British Surnames. Routledge & Keegan Paul.
2. Ibid.

garlic, tansy and so forth. But these could be home grown, if not locally gathered. **Pepper** is also to be found as an occasional nickname for this same merchant. Looking into the spicer's shop, we may indeed see one of the buyers from the household of another wealthy merchant, scrutinising the goods before purchase. This servant's position in his master's house has produced the surname **Purves** (also **Purvis** etc), a relic of the French 'purveier', 'to provide'. He will be ordering ingredients for, among other dishes, a thick broth called 'pottage', which could contain many vegetables, meat, fish together with herbs and spices and was greatly enjoyed. The names **Pottage** and **Pottinger** have survived the centuries from the preparer of this well-liked dish.

Leeks, beans, peas, onions and cabbage were among the vegetables grown in garden plots and sold in markets throughout the summer months and, although they were smaller than our modern versions and rather differently flavoured, they were boiled with herbs and sometimes fruits, to make stews, or else they would be dried for winter use. The Old English word for vegetable was 'wyrt' and so, from the vegetable seller comes our surname **Wort**.

The maker and seller of butter must be one source of the rather uncommon surname **Butters**. Another source, however, was the keeper of the buttery, a cool room in the cellars of the better class houses, in which the wines and food were kept. Cheese too, was a favourite food and this was made and sold by the **Cheesewright** or **Cheeseman**.

Drink

Turning now from food to drink, we find that we have inherited just a few names associated with alcoholic beverages. Ale was the common drink, for, as in the countryside, water carried diseases and was avoided, unless boiled in stews. Although many households brewed their own ale, it was to the **Brewer** that most men turned when ale was wanted. It was largely due the brewer's business that drunkenness was commonplace, particularly in towns like London, where ale could cost as little as two pence a gallon (less than one penny in today's money). Men and women of all classes succumbed. There were many alehouses in the towns, sometimes having a stall outside, from which the 'ale-wives' sold their brews. It was mostly the women (the **Brewsters**) who brewed the ale, often all the year round, but traditionally in October, when the barley, wheat and oats were ready. When their brews were prepared and the civic ale-tasters were satisfied as to their quality, the women would raise their ale-stake or broom, outside their houses to advertise that the beverage was now to be had. Often, the alewife's cry would be 'Good ale!' and thus she unwittingly created the surname **Goodall**.

The tavern keeper has also left us with the names **Taverner**, **Inman** and **Ostler**, this last from the French 'ostelier', but in later centuries an ostler came to mean a stableman.

Mead was a sweet alcoholic drink that was made from fermented honey and had been known for many hundreds of years. However, the high cost of the honey required to make a gallon of mead meant that it was a drink largely enjoyed by the wealthy, who drank it from decorated vessels called mazers. The brewer of this splendid drink has given us one source of the surname **Meade** (the other origin of the name is the nickname applied to one who lived in or near a particular meadow).

Wine too, was an important drink, stored in wooden casks in the **Wynyard** – the wine-yard – by the **Vintner** (**Vinter** is a slightly more common version today) at the wharf where it had been unloaded after being shipped from the Continent.

One might reasonably expect **Beer** to have its origins in the brewing trade, but this is not so. The usual word for beer in mediæval times was 'ale', so that the surname **Beer** must refer to something else. In fact, it nearly always recalled someone from any of the several places in the West Country which had this word as part of the place name: Beer Hackett, Beer Charter and Beer Crocombe for example.

Finally, a mention of a non-alcoholic liquid, **Milk**. Although a familiar substance, there was nothing important about it, except perhaps its colour, that might ensure its survival as a surname. Happily, the name still exists, as about 60 entries in the national electoral database reveal. An early instance of the name is to be seen in a register of the Freemen of the City of York for the year 1367: 'William Mylk ....'[1]. It was probably most often applied to one with a particularly pale complexion or even a feeble manner.

Textiles

As I said in the section on 'Work in the village', a surprising number of our surnames owe their existence to the mediæval cloth-making industry. Indeed, of the current ten most common English surnames (**Smith**, **Taylor**, **Miller**, **Baker**, **Webb**, **Wright**, **Turner**, **Cooper**, **Walker** and **Mason**), three: **Taylor**, **Webb** and **Walker** are associated with the cloth craftsmen.

All the village cloth workers' skills were to be found in the towns, of course, but here we would also find the specialists, such as the worker who could make braid for the more costly clothes. This delicate work was done by the **Trinder** using a 'tryndelle', a sort of spindle to twist

---

1. P. H. Reaney (1979 edition) The Origin of English Surnames Routledge & Keegan Paul.

the threads. Similar work was done by the **Brader**, the **Corder** and the **Twiner**. The **Roper** and **Stringer** made their goods for a variety of uses, including bowstrings, while coarsely woven cloth for heavy duty work was produced by the **Sacker** (often seen as **Sachs** and **Sacks**).

The **Draper** and **Clothier** sold only the finished cloth, usually to other craftsmen, like the **Challenor**, whose speciality was a type of blanket called a 'chalonn'. The most costly textiles, however, were to found at the shop of the **Mercer** who, like the **Draper**, also sold most of his wares to other craftsmen who would then make up the cloth into clothes, some fine and intricately decorated, others simple and elegant.

The tailor (**Taylor**) was the general clothes maker and this name is currently second in the table of current surname frequency. In some districts, the word **Parmenter** (there are several spellings of this), from the French word for 'tailor', was preferred.

The **Hosier** made hose – like today's thick tights – and stockings, while the **Chaucer** made leather breeches (and probably hose). The wealthier classes liked their clothes trimmed and lined with fur and the artisan who carried out this work was the **Pilcher**. He would also make a complete fur robe for those who could afford such a pleasing luxury.

A small group of names taken from headwear might show occupational origins, or equally may have singled out the wearers: **Capp**, **Hatt**, **Hodd** and **Hood**. **Capper** and **Hatter** were certainly occupational in origin.

Before we leave the craftsman of the clothing trades, let's look briefly at the merchants themselves. In mediæval times, the dealer in general goods was the **Chapman**, a word which stemmed from the Old English word 'ceapmann'. The word, however, began to fall out of use after the Normans introduced their own word, **Merchant**, which, even so, tended be applied to the more worthy class of tradesman – a step up in commercial respectability.

The **Pedlar** (often **Pedder** today) was also introduced from the French 'pied de lievre' ('fleet of foot') and also helped to oust the native word **Chapman**.

Transport

The movement of goods over anything more than the small distances between neighbouring villages or across a town, was much more difficult than it is today, for no good roads had been built since Roman times and the routes which led across country were rutted and had fallen into universal decay. Even the tracks leading up to the city gates were usually in poor condition, though the civic authorities in most places did their best to keep the streets within the walls in a state of reasonable repair.

Loads that could not be carried on a person's back or across the shoulders, could be placed in the pannier baskets of a packhorse or a donkey, or drawn on an ox-cart or even a handcart, if such could be found. The **Tranter**, a pedlar of small general goods, would often be seen pushing a small handcart around the streets and calling his wares. If the **Tranter** could afford the cost of a horse, however, he could buy one from the **Cosser** or **Cozier**. Indeed, in 14th century Oxford, there existed a Horse-monger's Lane (on the site of present day Broad Street), indicating that the word 'horsemonger' was then in use for this tradesman. The London borough of Lambeth has a **Cosser** Street, as does the coastal town of Blyth in Northumberland, both of which may be ancient thoroughfares recalling the horse traders' dealings.

A man who carried goods for other people would soon find himself called the **Carter** or **Carrier**. The first is now a common surname, but the second is much less so, there being only 1 in my local telephone book, but 12 in the London directory. Since **Wain** was another word for waggon, it too has become a surname, together with its alternative spelling **Wayne**. The **Porter** was originally a door-keeper (from the French 'porte'), but the word, or the man, somehow began to signify a carrier of burdens and is always used this way today. The **Packman** too, was a mover of goods carried in his pack.

River transport was important, especially in London and a **Boater** must have carried goods up and down stream, while the **Ferriman** would row wares and passengers *across* the river. A **Marriner** and a **Seaman** were to be found on both coastal and seagoing vessels. The name **Galley** may once have referred to the rower of a boat, but it is also a contraction of 'galilee', a church porch and may recall one who lived near to the church entrance or who begged at the gate.

Building

In every town there was a regular need for craftsmen skilled in the arts of building, to keep structures in good repair and to construct new ones. The **Thatcher** (or **Thacker**) was seldom idle in a large town since, before about 1300, almost all houses and most other buildings were thatched. Thatched roofs were very vulnerable to fire, which could spread rapidly from roof to roof destroying whole streets in a very short time. London had suffered severe such devastations in 1077, 1087 and 1161, so that in 1189, the sheriff introduced regulations that would reduce the fire risk: tiles and slates were to be used where possible, instead of thatch. These decrees were extended in 1212 to compel builders to insert stone walls between adjoining wooden houses. **Tyler**, **Slater** and **Slatter** are names which arose from the new crafts. Although the most famous bearer of the name **Tyler** must be Wat Tyler, one of the leaders of the Peasants' Revolt of 1381, his is not the earliest recorded mention of the name: Dr Reaney[1] cites a Roger le Tuiler (1185) and a Simon le Tyeler (1296).

From the Old English word 'helian', meaning 'to cover', comes the surname **Helliar**, ultimately a tiler by trade. There are at least nine spellings of this name, including **Hilyar**.

The **Mason** would cut the stone to shape, while the **Carver** was the craftsman who executed the facings which, though of stone outside, were often of wood indoors. The **Waller** built the walls and was the mediæval equivalent of our bricklayer. He probably also daubed them with clay or whitewash to effect a weatherproof seal. Daubing, however, was the speciality of the **Dauber** in some districts and the **Clayer** (**Clare**) in others. Where expense was of little concern, the **Pargeter** was summoned to prepare and carve the plasterwork instead of the clay. He would sometimes cover the wet plaster with small stones or create highly decorative patterns, or simply leave the surface beautifully smooth and whitewashed.

Though glass had been known for over four thousand years, it was still an expensive commodity in mediæval times and was rarely found in town buildings. Coloured glass might be found in some churches and the plain, uncoloured glass could be afforded only by the wealthier classes, costing about 5 pence per square foot – an enormous price by 14th century standards. **Glass** was a nickname for the glass-maker himself, while **Glazier**, **Glazer** and **Glaze** were names earned by those who cut and fitted the panes using lead lattices.

Although bricks were only infrequently used at this time, the brick-maker is remembered in the name **Brick** (of which there are 20 listed in the London telephone directory).

The surname **Painter** usually referred to the house painter and decorator rather than the painter of pictures, but the unusual names **Artist** and **Artiss** are deceptive, for their origins lie in the town of Artois in France.

The Professions

In the middle ages, there were not many men of 'professional' standing, even in a city and so there are relatively few surnames recalling the professions. Perhaps the most common and the least expected, is **Barber**. He was mainly concerned with surgery and dentistry, hence the traditional red and white pole (representing blood and bandage) still to be seen outside some barbers' shops even today. The **Barber** has undoubtedly suffered a decline in status over the centuries!

---

1. P. H. Reaney (1976) A Dictionary of British Surnames. Routledge & Keegan Paul.

If the **Barber** was the surgeon, then the 'mire' was the physician. From this Old French word has come our surname **Myer**. **Myers** is the form we see more often today and recalls the one who served, or was apprenticed to, the physician. This is not the only origin of this name, however, since it has the more straightforward foundation in one who lived near a marsh or mire. The unusual surname **Physick** refers directly to the physician.

We would not today accord a fencing master the status of 'professional', in the same way that we would the doctor or lawyer, but I think we must credit his mediæval counterpart with this distinction. It is the case that officially, fencing schools in mediæval England were forbidden by law and we read of occasional prosecutions for breaches of the law in London – forty days imprisonment was the customary penalty. However, most town authorities usually turned a blind eye on the fencing establishments and on the tournaments enjoyed by the nobility. The fencing master was usually called by his French title of *l'escremissoer*, which became both **Skrimshaw** and **Scrimger** on the tongues of the English.

Two others whose professional services were in constant demand were the **Scrivener** and the **Latimer**. The first of these was often simply a clerk (from the French, 'écrire' – to write), but just as often he was an expert copier of books and manuscripts, since few outside the Church could write. The second of the two scholars was actually the 'latiner', who, as the word suggests, translated to and from Latin and wrote official records and documents in that language.

Town officers: the Law

To end this chapter about names arising from occupations, we must briefly look at the mediæval town officials, since we have inherited an important set of surnames from this group. If we begin with the highest ranking civic officer, we are faced with the **Sheriff**, which is a contraction of the words 'shire reeve' (see **Reeve** in the section, *Some Other Outdoor Occupations* in Chapter Two). The **Sheriff** was the king's personally appointed representative in each shire and was the chief administrator of justice. (We are reminded of the most famous sheriff of them all: the cunning adversary of Robin Hood, the Sheriff of Nottingham). Sheriffs were in positions of great power and sometimes they were corrupt and unscrupulous in the delivery of their judgements. There is a sheriff in each county today (and two in the City of London), but their modern duties are almost wholly ceremonial. The sheriff's deputy was the **Bailiff**, a much grander figure than the manorial **Bailiff** we met in the section about the village. This man was the chief municipal officer of the district or the chief justice under the sheriff and we have evolved almost a dozen variations on this name, from **Bailyff** to **Baly**.

In addition to these two high ranking civic officials, there were several executive officers of lower rank whose allegiance was to the courts. Firstly, the word **Beadle** (giving us **Biddle**) seems to have been a term freely used of several functionaries, including the bailiff's constable, his so-called 'tipstaff' and even in some towns, the court messenger. His official responsibilities included the carrying out of summonses and collecting fines. Next comes the **Sergeant**, whose duties were similar to those of the **Beadle**, though in some places, he may have been regarded as of a rather lesser presence.

The Church Court had its own equivalent of the **Beadle** or **Sergeant** in the form of the **Proctor**. Oxford University also adopted this title for two officers, first appointed in 1248, as enforcers of discipline within the student body.

Sumner is a natural rendering of the title 'summoner', an officer who summoned attendance at court those who were to receive judgment. His must have been an unpopular occupation, though few summoners could have been as repulsive as the one Chaucer describes in his Canterbury Tales.

In the London telephone book **Judge** outnumbers **Justice** by more than 4 to 1. However, the Isle of Man judiciary still preserves an Old English word for judge, albeit in its feminine form, **Deemster**. The mediæval pronouncer of judgments was the **Deemer** and this is occasionally found as a modern surname. These two forms are easily outnumbered in modern frequency by the alternative feminine **Dempster**.

The surname **Corner** occurs more often than one might expect and is, in some cases, a relic of the office of coroner, which was established in about the year 1200 by King John in order more efficiently to manage the royal revenues. The mediæval coroner was probably second only in importance to the **Sheriff**. It is more likely to be the case, however, that **Corner** recalls one whose dwelling was at the corner of a lane, field or some such location.

Finally, a mention of a few of the more humble public servants. The **Crier** was the broadcaster of news and an important source of local information to the citizens, since there was no other means of publishing messages and few could read. The **Waite** and the **Wakeman** were wardens who carried bugles or horns to sound the watches and alarms of the night, while the **Burgess** was a freeman of the borough, having first risen to a respected position of master craftsman or guild officer and as such, was granted considerable freedom from many of the obligations which bound other men. He was also able to benefit from royal charters that permitted certain concessions to the body of municipal burgesses.

Here we must bring to an end our look at surnames which have come down to us from the vast array of occupations performed by the English men and women of the 11th, 12th and 13th centuries, both in the village settlements and in the towns. Mediæval occupations have proved to be a rich source of our names and I have dealt with several hundred in this chapter, but there are many others unmentioned.

Chapter 3

Surnames from Places

"Neither was there, or is there, any town, village, hamlet,
or place in England, but hath made names to families."
William Camden, 'Remains' 1605

Perhaps the above quotation from William Camden's book would turn out to be a slightly exaggerated claim, but you can see Camden's point. Indeed, Camden himself possessed just such a surname! This statement is anyway, perhaps rather less true today than it was in 1605. This is because over the last century or so, several 'new towns' have been established, notably Stevenage, Letchworth and Welwyn in Hertfordshire, Peterlee in Durham, Milton Keynes in Buckinghamshire and Bourneville in Warwickshire. However, with the exceptions of Bourneville (built in 1894-5) and Peterlee (post-second world war), which were entirely new, the others had well-established villages as their foundations – even Milton Keynes is mentioned in a document of 1227-8.

The only surname I have been able to trace (other than **Milton**) that has its origin in any of these places is **Stevenage**. It is rare: there is now only 1 in the London electoral archive and none in the telephone book. However, leaving the 'new towns' aside, we can imagine, as Camden says, that most places must have been applied as additional names at some time, however briefly, with most of them disappearing several hundreds of years ago. It is also a fact that there are surnames in use today which signify places that cannot be found on any modern map. The explanation of this is that, after the main surname-forming period, a large number of villages were abandoned or depopulated for various reasons, eventually leaving behind little or no visible trace. Even their approximate location is uncertain in some cases: **Eccersley**, **Insall**, **Postlethwaite**, **Smithwick** and **Trefusis** are examples. These are still found as modern surnames – unfortunately their only vestige and memorial. If you were to discover that your surname seemed to be that of a lost village, it would certainly be worthwhile investigating further: the cause and date of the settlement's extinction and how many other people having the same name as yours are traceable. City libraries are helpful here, since they will have copies of all mainland telephone directories, which also give clues as to where the concentrations of a given surname are to be found. Of course, the Internet now has become an invaluable modern tool in searching for names.

It is interesting to examine the reasons for the disappearance of villages over the centuries. The first cause of extinction that will come to mind is disease. Most villages were virtually closed communities in the middle ages, having little or no contact with strangers and only perhaps an occasional trek to a nearby town market to buy or sell wares would lead to mixing with outsiders. Infections amongst the inhabitants could therefore spread catastrophically and could wipe out a small community, as happened in Tilgarsley near Eynsham in Oxfordshire. This village was deserted by 1350, while Tusmore, five miles to the north of Bicester (also Oxfordshire), '… had no soul remaining', according to tax commissioners sent there in 1355. These villages were indeed depopulated as a result of 'the pestilence' (the black death) which swept across England in the autumn of 1348, wiping out over a million people – about a third of the population. It reappeared, though with diminished intensity, in the years 1356, 1361, 1368 and 1391. Neither Tilgarsley nor Tusmore is listed as a surname in the current London telephone directory, nor are the names to be found in the British electoral records. So it seems that if they ever existed as surnames, they have vanished.

Another constant fear was famine due to crop failure. Unfavourable weather in the growing and harvesting seasons, or the wrong choice of crops, could mean starvation for many peasants, accompanied by the dwindling of the numbers in the village until there was no one left. Such disastrous famines were recorded in 1082, 1087, 1096, 1124 and 1125. If two consecutive harvests failed in the same districts, the effects on the local peasantry would be calamitous. Indeed, the dates just mentioned show an alarming regularity of failure.

As the years passed, the demand for wool for the expanding weaving industry grew enormously. Landlords in the Midlands and Cotswold districts saw that this demand could be very profitably satisfied by increasing their sheep flocks. An obvious move, therefore, was to evict peasants from certain villages and hamlets, usually without warning or recompense, level the cottages and turn the cornfields over to sheep pasture. The villages of Chalford, near Chipping Norton and Fawsley, about eight miles north of Banbury, both Cotswold settlements, were forcibly depopulated by 1485 for the sake of increased sheep grazing. Both Chalford and Fawsley are absent from the London telephone books and the electoral registers, suggesting that they too probably no longer exist as surnames.

A fourth cause of mediæval village annihilation was the encroach-ment of the sea. About twenty settlements on the coast of Yorkshire were claimed in this way during the 13th century. This sort of geographical change, however, would account for the loss of only a few villages countrywide.

There are other minor reasons for abandonment, especially of hamlets, the only one of any significance being the gradual demise of the few inhabitants, leaving Nature to embrace the poor crofts and tracks.

In 14th century London, there were to be found hundreds of individuals bearing surnames, of a sort, representing towns and villages all over England. How could this be? Peasants were bound to their lord and his land and could not leave it without his permission and anyway, most villeins would not wish to venture away from their own familiar localities. The lord would usually grant consent for one person to marry another from a neighbouring village on his manor and for the couple to take up permanent residence in one or other of the villages, but, as a rule, peasants expected to remain in their native or chosen village for life. It is certainly true that a bold fellow might run away to a town or city for whatever reason, knowing that, if he could remain undiscovered for a year and a day, he could retain his freedom. However, he would be foolish to reveal the name of his home village before his year was up for fear of word reaching the ears of his master's bailiff. Before the time was expired, he may have acquired some sort of nickname anyway, if not prompted by the unaccustomed intonation of his speech, then from some aspect of his appearance. **Newman** and **Newcome** would often suffice for the occasional stranger who seemed to have come to stay. However, this sort of occurrence does not seem to explain why so many place-names appeared in London so quickly. A more convincing explanation is that the sons of freemen and independent landholders, who were not bound to the land, would look towards the cities for a living and perhaps some excitement too, in the same way that today's youth will often be drawn to the bright lights of the cities in the hope of pleasure and fortune. I think it must have been largely these young men who carried their identities into the towns and cities, thus helping to spread a variety of surnames across the face of England. To this group we can add the small number of villeins who had suffered eviction by sheep-rearing landlords, or who had been forced to forsake their homes for other reasons mentioned earlier and, being without work and food, in desperation found their ways to nearby towns and cities. Inevitably, many of these newcomers would be called after their villages of origin.

Over the intervening centuries, many spellings have been so changed through dialectic evolution and speech peculiarities that it is sometimes not obvious that a surname is derived from a place name. For example, **Dossett** is really **Dorset**, **Bruckshaw** is a distortion of **Birkenshaw** in Yorkshire and Strathclyde, **Hebborn** can be **Hepburn** in Northumberland and **Pizey** is a transformation of **Pusey** in Berkshire. Very often, however, place names have tell-tale endings which betray their origins and we are used to this idea, for place-names represent a substantial proportion of surnames which are familiar to us.

Here is a list of the most frequently encountered suffixes which will signify a place or a local feature:

-borough	– a fortified place, as in Longborough (Gloucestershire);
-bury	– a defended or fortified settlement, as in **Bradbury** (Cleveland);
-by	– Danish for settlement, as in **Dunsby** (Lincolnshire);
-chester	– Old English 'ceaster': a fort or encampment, as in Ribchester (Lancs);
-cliff	– a slope or cliff, as in **Ratcliff** (Middlesex) ;
-combe	– a narrow valley, as in **Seacombe** (Merseyside);
-cot	– a dwelling or cottage, as in **Burcot** (Oxfordshire);
-dale	– a valley, as in **Dinsdale** (Durham);
-den	– a small, shallow valley, as in **Norden** (Dorset);
-don	– a hill, as in **Headon** (Lincolnshire);
-ey(e)	– an island, as in **Pusey** (Berkshire);
-field	– a noteworthy field, as in **Duffield** (Derbyshire);
-ford	– a shallow river crossing, as in **Bamford** (Lancashire);
-ham	– a village, meadow settlement, as in **Woodham** (Essex);
-hurst	– a wooded hill, as in **Lyndhurst** (Hampshire);
-ley	– a clearing, as in **Handley** (Cheshire);
-low	– a small hill or mound, as in **Harlow** (Essex);
-ness	– a headland or promontory, as in **Holderness** (Yorkshire);
-shaw	– a wood, as in **Openshaw** (Lancashire);
-stead	– a place, as in **Felstead** (Essex);
-stock	– a place, as in **Bostock** (Cheshire);
-thorpe	– a hamlet or farmstead, as in **Calthorpe** (Norfolk);
-ton	– an enclosure or settlement, as in **Holton** (Oxfordshire);
-well	– a stream or well, as in **Colwell** (Devon);
-wick	– a farm settlement, as in **Stanwick** (Northamptonshire);
-wood	– a wood, as in **Harwood** (Durham);
-worth	– an enclosure or homestead, as in **Pebworth** (Buckinghamshire).

Most of these endings have formed surnames on their own account without a preceding element and several of them have similar meanings: **Dale** and **Combe**, for instance which, together with **Clough** and **Bottoms**, referred to valleys of different kinds, while **Thorpe** (often transformed in the peculiar English way into **Throp**), **Wick** and **Worth**, together with **Croft** and **Stead**, come from words which, at first, meant a specifically farming settlement or dwelling, but later came to suggest simply a village or hamlet.

Bury or **Berry** come from the Old English word 'byrig', which meant more than just a settlement, rather a defended or fortified place or even a stronghold. A clearing in a wood is indicated by **Lee**, **Lea**, **Leigh** and **Thwaite**, though this last can sometimes have its origin in an Old Norse word meaning 'meadow'. The Old English word for a meadow was 'ham(m)', but unfortunately, it is very difficult to distinguish it in its compounds from another Old English word, 'ham', which meant village or settlement. Both **Hamm** and **Ham** occur as surnames today (there are 27 instances of **Hamm** and 10 of **Ham** in the London telephone directory). A dwelling near to a small hill or a mound might well have earned its occupant the nickname **Low** or **Law**, from the Old English word for a hill, 'hlaw', while a wooded hill was a **Hurst** (giving **Hirst**) and a thicket of trees was indicated by **Grove** and **Grave**. **Rigg** recalled one who chose to live high up on a ridge above the village.

Continuing our examination of tell-tale suffixes, which have themselves become surnames in their own right, we might now glance at a small group that have to do with water. First, three names coming from words which meant spring or stream are **Brook**, **Fleet** and **Wells**. A dweller near a brook might easily attract that word as a nickname, but **Fleet**, although meaning a stream (or even an estuary), can have as its origin one from **Fleet** in Hampshire. To confuse matters more, **Fleet** was a nickname sometimes given to one who was fleet of foot. **Wells** could also have a connection with the Somerset city of Wells, of course. In its singular form, **Well** is still occasionally found – there is currently one entry in the London telephone book and 10 more are to be found on the London electoral register. It most commonly occurs, however, in compounds like **Atwell** and **Foxwell**.

A **Holme** was a small island in a fen or was surrounded by streams, while **Moore** and **More** could mean the fen itself, as well as the higher moorland. **Fenn**, though nearly always a prefix, recalled a dweller near a **Marsh**, but could also refer to one from a place of that name in either Lincolnshire or Devon.

There are 868 entries of **Ford** in the London telephone directory and this is not surprising, since there are at least ten counties in which places of this name are still to be found, as well as the hundreds of place names having the word as their suffix, like **Bamford**, **Oxford** and **Stamford**. The word **Forth**, a variation of **Ford**, occurs occasionally alone as a surname, but it is more often seen as a suffix: **Stanforth** and **Spofforth** for instance. They all alluded to the familiar shallow river crossing place.

Ing on its own, may recall an ancient local village elder or leader of that name, but it is usually seen as the suffix '-ing' of a personal name or as a central syllable within a name (**Birmingham**, **Pennington**). There are many occurrences of the suffix form: **Downing** (and **Dunning**), **Stebbing** and **Tipping** are examples. In such names as these it will indicate 'the family of ....' or 'the people of ...', so that **Dunning** would mean 'of the people of Dunn' and **Stebbings**, 'one of Stybba's people'. Of

course, there is nothing known about these community leaders and in a
good many cases we are left to surmise the exact form of the man's name
from the form of the surname fragment. **Tilling** must refer to one called
Tylli or Tilla and **Lucking** probably to a man called Leofeca. However,
not all of the prefixes are remnants of someone's personal name: **Horning**
meant 'the people at the bend (of the river, track etc)'. There are so many
alternatives involving '-ing' that one really needs a small library of reference works at one's elbow to have any chance of determining a given
meaning; even Dr Reaney admits that his great dictionary is far from
complete.

We cannot leave the '-ing' theme quite yet for, sooner or later, we are
bound to come across names in which the '-ing-' syllable appears in the
middle of the name. Such names will usually have a distinct place-name
look to them, though we may never have heard of the place itself. It will
be the tell-tale final element that will give the game away, being most
often '-ham' or '-ton', although '-holm', '-thorp,' '-ley', and others crop up
occasionally. The Old English word 'tun' is the origin of our word 'town'
and meant an enclosed settlement or village and, in the form of the suffix
'-ton', appears in many hundreds of place British place-names. 'Ham'
was of a similar meaning to 'tun', but sometimes with the additional
allusion to a meadow location. Examples of this sort of surname are:

Ellington (Kent)	– the settlement of Ealda's people;
Harrington (Cumbria)	– the settlement of Haefra's people;
Horsington (Lincolnshire)	– the settlement of Horsa's people;
Pilkington (Lancashire)	– the settlement of Pileca's people;
Buckingham (Buckinghamshire)	– the village of Bucca's folk;
Massingham (Norfolk)	– the village of Mæssa's folk;
Passingham (Northamptonshire)	– the village of Passa's folk (the place is now called Passenham);
Tushingham (Cheshire)	– the village of Tunsiga's folk.

There are obviously many names in this form and one cannot do
better than to refer to Professor Ekwall's excellent place-name dictionary[1]
for detailed information on them. Of course, the fact that surnames have
the endings '-ington' or '-ingham' simply indicates that a mediæval
ancestor originated in that place rather than that he was in any way
related to the headman whose personal name begins the word.

Before moving onto the influence of the Danes on our surnames,
I'll mention a few 'stand-alone' surnames derived from places. An
Old Danish name is Asbiorn ('god-bear') and is one origin of **Osborne**
(another source of the name is 'stream near the sheep'). **Hails** too, has

---

1 Ekwall E. (1960 Ed.) Concise Oxford Dictionary of Place Names. Clarendon
Press.

some stream connections, as well as being place-names in Scotland and Gloucestershire. **Newbold** (also **Newbald** and **Newboult**), meaning 'new building' also occurs in many place-names. **Cardy** is an interesting shortening of the Cumberland place **Cardew** ('black fort') and **Hesketh** is a rendering of the Old Scandinavian 'hestaskeið', which reminds us that those northern people enjoyed the sport of horse-racing!

Those place-names that end in '-by' are the consequence of the settlement of the Scandinavian invaders in the east and north-east of England during the 9th, 10th and early 11th centuries (see Figure 1 for the extent of Danish influence). The suffix' -by' was generally equivalent to the English '-tun' and meant a village or farming settlement and generated place names like **Hornby** ('Horni's settlement') and **Darby** ('village near

Figure 1. The extent of the Danish occupation of England and Wales from the 9th century.

the deer' – identical to **Derby**).

In the two centuries before the Norman Conquest, Scandinavian invaders settled in the East Midlands and north-east of England. The map on the previous page shows the extent of that settlement, usually referred to as 'Danelaw'. Two exceptions to the main body of the Danelaw are Tenby in South Wales and Kirby Cross (with Kirby le Soken) in Essex – both difficult to spot until you look very carefully at the map! The 48 places indicated on the map all include the characteristic Danish suffix '-by', but they by no means represent the total number of such places in the region.

There were 543 settlements recorded in Domesday (1086) that had the Danish suffix '-by'. Many of these names were simple modifications of the existing villages' English names in order to make them more easily pronounceable by the occupying Danes. **Badby** (Badda's stronghold) in Northamptonshire is an instance of this. This place was originally 'Baddan byrig' (approximately 'Badabury') in its pre-Viking days, but by the time of Domesday it had lost its Old English 'byrig' and had assumed the characteristic Danish suffix (Badebi in Domesday). We can see that by the middle of the 11th century the Danish influence was extensive.

Two other important suffixes are '-den' and '-don', each originating in the Old English words 'denu' (a shallow valley) and 'dun' (a hill). They have turned themselves into today's **Dean** and **Down** and retain their original meanings. The prefix to both '-den' and '-don' may be either a form of personal name or the recognition of some local feature: **Hunsdon** (Hertfordshire) is the 'hill of Hun' and **Baldon** (Oxfordshire) is 'Bealda's hill', while **Bradden** (Northamptonshire) means 'broad valley' and **Wilsden** (West Yorkshire) is the 'valley of the people of Wilsige'. However, **Headon** (Nottinghamshire) means 'high hill' and **Haddon** (Derbyshire) is 'heather hill'. In many names, of course, the independent word 'hill' itself forms the ending, as in **Harthill** (hill of the stags – Cheshire). An Ordnance Survey map of any part of England will reveal many more of these interesting names and Professor Ekwall's Dictionary will probably do the rest.

Many place-name endings, such as '-bridge', '-borough', '-beck', '-hall' and '-land' speak clearly for themselves, largely because they also exist as independent words in current use, but there are places whose names often have only one syllable and we are left without any clues as to their significance: **Lobb**, **Kenn** and **Beale** are three. The first was Old English for 'spider' and may have been an individual's nickname in some cases, but this meaning cannot be correct for the places of this name in Devon and Oxfordshire, where it seems to have indicated a steep hill. **Kenn** is a stream-name in both Somerset and Derbyshire and meant 'white, brilliant'. **Beale** has a number of possible origins – 'bee hill' in Northumberland, 'corner by the river bends' in Yorkshire and possibly the French 'belle', meaning beautiful.

A common reminder of the Roman occupation of Britain is to be found in the many names which incorporate some form of the Latin word 'castra', meaning a fort or defended encampment. As a suffix, this word appears in several forms: -caster, -cester, -chester and occasionally -kester. The early English also used a similar word 'ceaster' as a description of a closed community. **Chester** itself must clearly mean a fortified military camp, but this is not the earliest name of the city, for the 1st century Romans called it Deva Victrix, which must have referred to its location on the River Dee. **Lancaster** may look as if it ought to mean 'the long camp', but this distinction is held by **Lanchester**, as is clearly shown by its 12th century spelling, 'Langecestr'. **Lancaster**, being situated on the River Lune, really meant 'fort on the Lune'.

Mediæval town dwellers had more freedom of movement and residence than their village counterparts and by moving from one town to another, they carried the name of their town or city of origin with them in many cases. So let's look now at some of the surnames that are also town and city names.

London must claim precedence here, I suppose, since its history extends at least to the Roman settlement of Londinium in the 2nd century. As a surname, it is rather a poor performer, with only 51 entries in the London telephone directory and 147 other listings in national electoral registers. Thus the surname is not as common as we might expect for so important a place, perhaps because, as the city grew in size and self-sufficiency, its citizens felt very little need to settle elsewhere. **Birmingham**, rather surprisingly, outdoes **London** in my local 'phone book with 4 entries against none for **London**! The London telephone book has 27 **Birmingham** entries. It is one of those names containing the syllables '-ing-' and '-ham', which we looked at earlier and means 'settlement of Beorma's folk', its spelling having changed only a little since the Domesday entry (Bermingeham).

Manchester, like **London**, is not all that common a surname nowadays. It is also rather obscure in meaning and we can really only speculate on the origin of the first syllable, which may have come from the Latin 'mamma' – a breast, implying a 'fort on the breast-shaped hill'.

Leicester is encountered in several forms, including **Laister**, **Lassiter** and **Lester**, this last one being the most common by far. Its meaning though, is a bit of a puzzle for, although there is the familiar '-cester' suffix, this seems to have been a development of the late 9th century. The Romans' name for the place was Ratæ Coritanorum (the settlement of the Corieltauvi tribe). This, together with the fact that a nearby river was called the Leire, makes it pretty certain that it meant 'people dwelling near the River Leire'.

Norwich and its alternative surname spelling, **Norridge**, are forms of 'north wick', meaning a farming settlement to the north.

Wakefield is either the 'field belonging to Waca' or the field where the annual festival of wakes plays was held.

Kendal is very straightforward: it means 'Kent dale' – valley of the River Kent, on which this pleasant town stands.

The surname **Carlisle** is found in small numbers in our telephone books, but it is yet another place whose meaning is uncertain. It may be that the Welsh word 'caer', meaning 'a city', is the first element of the name and Luguvalos (the name of the leader of the settlement) is the second, giving the 'city of Luguvalos'. An alternative explanation is 'place of the god Lugus'. If these interpretations look a little improbable, it simply goes to show that there is still much scholarly uncertainty about the name.

By contrast with the last mentioned name, **Bedford** is easy: 'Bedda's ford' across the Great Ouse and known as such since at least the 9th century.

The larger cities, it seems, are less likely to have perpetuated their names than the smaller settlements and towns. Some places seem to have little encouragement for perpetuity: Wolverhampton and Middlesbrough for instance, though both places have long histories stretching far beyond the surname-forming period. The first springs from the 'high settlement of Wulfrun' ('Wulfrun heantune'), while the second meant simply the 'middle settlement'. Having so many syllables certainly makes such place-names cumbersome and alternative personal nicknames would soon be found.

Having now ascended from the smaller features of the countryside: the wells, fords, clearings, valleys and so on, through the settlements and encampments, to the towns and cities, it seems sensible to step up to the top-but-one rung of the ladder and look at the occurrence of the shire-names as surnames.

We might be tempted to reason that shire-names ought to be rarer than city-names as surnames, since people moving from one place to another would have been unlikely to have carried a name with them that represented anything as large as a shire, unless the move was a very significant one, say from Yorkshire to London. In such a case, the difference in speech, rather than the shire-name might have been the more likely cause of comment. We must not forget that it was usually other people in the neighbourhood and workplace who gave the newcomer his nickname. (An old Welsh friend of mine who lived in Kent, always referred to one of her well-established neighbours as 'the Gloucester woman'). A glance into the London telephone books reveals that 21 of the old shires are featured as surnames, with **Kent** (370) by far the most common and **Wiltshire** (122) coming next. Of the other 19, **Durham** (71) and **Cornwall** (57) are in numbers greater than 50. There is, by contrast, but a single entry for **Yorkshire**. It is likely that such long names as Northamptonshire, Huntingdonshire and Herefordshire were either shortened or were never bothered with.

Finally, to end this section, what of country-based names? **England** and **English** (**Inglis** being the more common Scottish form of the word) are known in small numbers and must have been the result of Englishmen living amongst the Scots, Welsh and even the Danes (who occupied a large part of 11th century England). Such surnames as **Scott**, **Scotland**, **Walsh** and **Welch** must have arisen in the same way – descriptions of these foreigners living amongst the English.

Surnames from France and its neighbours

It is largely due to the conquering Normans in the middle of the 11th century, that their recently adopted custom of adding a descriptive name to their personal name was copied by (or impressed upon) the English over the next three centuries. It is hardly surprising therefore, that many French place-names found their way into England, eventually to become surnames. Many of these names arrived with the Normans in 1066, or soon afterwards and were gradually spread over the face of the land as King William made gifts of estates to his loyal countrymen. Suddenly, native Englishmen were hearing new and strange sounding names in their localities and were soon making their own faltering attempts at the pronunciation of their new masters' names: Guy d'Oilly, Geoffrey de Mandeville, Guy de Raimbeaucourt for example. Over the next three centuries, many other French names were introduced into the language, as trade with the near Continent increased and foreign merchants established themselves in England's principal cities and ports.

The most natural and obvious way of referring to a foreigner was by his country of origin, such as **France**, **French**, **German**, **Holland** and **Spain**.

By far the greater number of foreign names came from France of course and their bearers were usually known after the province or district from which they came. Here are the major French provinces and the English surnames, in their modern forms, with which they are associated:

Angou........	**Angwin**;	Goelle........	**Gower**;
Artois.........	**Artiss**, **Artist**;	Maine........	**Maine**;
Brittany......	**Brett**, **Brittain**, **Britten**;	Picardy.......	**Picard**, **Power**, **Poore** (this from Poix);
Burgundy..	**Burgoyne**, **Burling**;	Poitou........	**Peto**.

The five Départments of the ancient Channel province of Normandy have been the sources of most surnames from French places and it is the Départment of Calvados that has provided rather more than any other. Here are some of the surnames in use today that have their origins in places in Calvados:

Beamish from Beaumais-sur-Dive;
Blomfield from Blomville-sur-Mer;
Bruce from Le Brus;
Bursey from Burcy;
Cane from Caen;
Curzon from Notre-Dame-de-Courson;
Dansey from Aisny;
Disney from Isigny;
Doyley from Ouilly-le-Basset;
Loach from Les Loges;
Montgomery from Sainte-Foy-de-Montgommery;
Percy from Percy-en-Auge;
Tracey from Tracy-Bocage.

Surnames that originated in the other Départments of Normandy are also plentiful. Here are some of them, with the Départment in brackets:

Beecham from Beauchamp (La Manche);
Beaumont from Beaumont-le-Roger (Eure);
Burney, **Burnie** from Bernay (Eure);
Bullen, **Boleyn** from Boulogne (Pas-de-Calais);
Gamage from Gamaches (Eure);
Grenfell, **Grenville** from Grainville-la-Teintureiere (Seine-Inférieure);
Harcourt from Harcourt (Eure);
Lyons from Lyons-la-Forêt (Eure);
Manners from Mesniers (Seine-Inférieure);
Montague from Montaigu (La Manche);
Mortimer from Mortemer-sur-Eaulne (Seine-Inférieure);
Mobray from Montbrai (La Manche);
Pacey from Pacy-sur-Eure (Eure);
Venables from Venables (Eure);
Vernon from Vernon (Eure);
Warren from La Varenne (Seine-Inférieure).

These lists are very short and give only a few of the many hundreds of names that derive from French places.

There are many fewer surnames that have their roots in Belgian towns, however. Four of the most commonly encountered are **Brabham** (from Brabant), **Danvers** (from Antwerp), **Bridges** (from Bruges) and **Gaunt** (from Ghent). The word **Fleming** of course, would have described one from **Flanders** (once a free state, but now a district of Belgium).

From the German towns of Cologne and Lübeck come our surnames **Cullen** and **Lubbock**, while Portugal has been the source of **Pettingell**. The surname **Denmark** is also occasionally found.

This journey through surnames from places has been interesting and instructive and has also shown just how many of our names were imports. This means too, that those of us bearing a surname that originated abroad are very likely to have had a foreign ancestor in Mediæval England – an intriguing thought.

Chapter 4

Surnames from Local Features

The mediæval peasant was an observant and inventive individual and readily labelled his fellows with descriptive names, flattering and insulting (at least to our modern delicate sensibilities), pleasing and coarse, or just harmless. All of these names were of course, true nicknames of one sort or another, and those I have called 'harmless' often include reference to the location of a person's dwelling: at the edge of a wood, beneath a hill or by a bend in the river. Every feature of the English landscape seems to have come in for a mention: woods, meadows, trees, streams, gates, hills, valleys, bends, crossroads, churches, bridges, hedges, ditches and many more. Our surnames arising from local features do indeed form a large and interesting group.

An easy way to identify or locate a particular individual is to state his or her personal name and follow it with the words 'at the' or 'by the' and then the closest local feature to his or her dwelling. For example, 'Robert at the wood', which in normal speech will soon be reduced to Robert Attewood, and indeed, this is often how we find such names recorded in early mediæval documents. Subsequently, the '-e-' was lost in many cases, as was a '-t-', though some of the names listed here are to be found in all three forms.

The meaning of **Attwood** (and **Atwood)** (93)[1] is obvious and **Attlee** (and **Atlee**) (6) could have the same meaning, or else 'at the clearing in the wood'. Other self-explanatory names are **Athill** (and **Atthill**) (11), **Attfield** (and **Atfield**) (28), **Atree** (and **Attree**) (18), **Attridge** (**Atridge)** (25), **Attwater** (**Atwater**) (10) and **Attwell** (**Atwell**) (39). The surname **Attenborough** (20) is less obvious, but its meaning becomes clearer when

---

1. Numbers in brackets refer to the entries in the London telephone directories at the time of the research.

we look at its alternative spelling **Attenbarrow**, 'dweller by the mound or hill'. Occasionally we will come across names that have lost the '-t-' sound completely, like **Allaun** (0), 'at the glade', **Achurch** (1), 'at the church', **Ahearne** (27), 'at the corner' and **Agutter** (3), 'at the ditch'. We will recall that one of Robin Hood's men was called Allan **Adale** (0), 'at the valley': the complete absence of this name from the national electoral registers would suggest that it no longer exists.

Another prefix used to pinpoint someone was 'By-'. Such local features as a **Ford**, **Waters**, **Field** and **Wood** all acquired this syllable: **Byford** (36), **Bywaters** (27), **Byfield** (29) and **Bywood** (0), though none of these is all that common, as can be seen. **Bycroft** (0) and **Byard** (8) both meant 'dweller by the enclosure', while **Bygrave** (36) referred to one who dwelt near a grove of trees. **Byfleet** (1) recalls a 'dweller by the stream', unless the person's place of origin was **Byfleet**, a hamlet that grew up around a stream in Surrey.

Some unusual and delightful members of this group are **Bythesea** (pronounced 'Bithersee'), **Bytheseashore** (pronounced 'Bitherseashore'), **Bytheway** and **Bysouth**, all of which speak charmingly for themselves. I can find no trace of the first two of these in any mainland telephone directory, so their survival is now in question, but the last two do still occur in very small numbers throughout Britain.

The last prefix of any importance we will look at is 'Under-'. **Underhill** (33) and **Underdown** (13) both meant 'at the foot of the hill', while **Underwood** (172) may well have recalled the man who lived 'beneath the wooded hill' or simply 'in the wood'. The name **Underhay** (5) is an uncommon surname nowadays. It is from the Old English word 'hæg' and meant an enclosure of some sort, or sometimes just a hedge or fence, so that the name must have been acquired by one who lived or worked next to such a feature.

Woods and trees occur very frequently in our surnames and have done so from an early period. One of the most familiar trees to a mediæval Englishman was the oak and this tree, in various guises, yields quite a few surnames: **Oak** (2), **Oakes** (26), **Attock** ('at the oak') (0 in the London telephone book, though 14 are listed in electoral rolls), **Nock** ('atten oak') (1), **Noakes** (32), **Nokes** (6), **Rock(e)** (21), **Roake** (4) and even **Rook(e)** (4).

The ash tree has given us even more surnames than the oak, probably more than twenty, among which are **Ash(e)** (47) itself, **Nash** ('atten ash') (129) and **Dash** (11). The surname **Nash** is by far the most common. There are several compounds which begin with the prefix 'Ash-': **Ashfield** (5) (there are several places of this name), **Ashcroft** ('dweller by the pasture or enclosure with the ash tree') (21), **Ashwood** (also a village in Staffordshire) (3) and **Ashley** (many place names include this word which means an ash meadow or wood) (87).

Other trees which provide us with familiar surnames are **Birch** (99),

Beech (30), **Hazel** (18), and **Hawthorn(e)** (30). **Elms** (27) is less often met, while **Rowan** (59) and its companion **Rountree** (7), that is 'rowan tree', are also out of the ordinary. The alder, pear and holly trees have left us a substantial legacy between them in **Alder** (34), **Perry** (157) and **Hollis** (37), once again demonstrating that to have lived close to a prominent tree, whatever its type, was likely to have brought forth a n appropriate after-name. The willow has also bequeathed us its name, but in its more ancient guise of **Sallow** (0 in the London 'phone book, but 4 examples survive nationally). The names **Sallows** (3) and **Sallis** (1) are variations. The yew tree is one source of the surname **Yeo** (another is associated with a nearby stream).

Although they are not trees of course, brambles would have been a common sight in hedges and on banks and their blackberries would have introduced a welcome source of sweetness into the autumn diet of many a villager. One who lived among the bramble bushes would have earned himself the name of **Briars** (2), **Briers** (4) or **Bramble** (15). Dr Reaney[1] mentions such a man recorded in Huntingdonshire, 'John in le Breres', in the year 1279. **Sedge** (0) too, appears in our names occasionally, as does **Sedgeman** (the name given to a thatcher in some localities) (1).

Enclosed land was usually bounded by a hedge (Old English 'haeg') and one whose dwelling was close to such a feature might well attract the nickname **Hedge(s)** or **Hay**. **Hayes** too, may have meant the same, though it also arises from one who originated in one of the many places of that name (Kent, Middlesex, Warwickshire, Somerset and Sussex for example).

Other surnames which have arisen from residence near to a conspicuous local feature include **Pool**, **Stone**, **Brook** (**Burn** is the northern and Scottish word for this), **Rivers**, **Marsh**, **Hill**, **Meadows**, **Greenfield**, **Heath** and **Cross**. Also **Pile** (**Pyle**) and **Stubbs** refer to one who lived near to, or against a prominent stake or tree stumps. **Broadbent** referred to one whose dwelling was on a wide, grassy plain or heath (broad + 'beonet', Old English for a grassy moor), while **Broomfield** recalls either a dweller near a field of broom, or one whose origin was one of several places of that name. In addition, some of these names acquired the Old English suffix '-man', as if to identify more emphatically the person in question: **Pullman** ('pool man'), **Brookman**, **Hillman**, **Crossman**, though **Bateman** signifies the 'servant of Bate' (that is Bartholomew).

Some ancient words that have all but disappeared from our modern everyday speech have, fortunately, been preserved in some of our familiar surnames: **Holt** was an Old English word for a wood, as well as being a common element in place-names in at least six counties and **Sykes**, from the word 'sīc', referred to small streams. **Bourne**, too was a stream (**Burn**

---

1. P. H. Reaney (1976 edition) A Dictionary of British Surnames. Routledge & Keegan Paul.

in Scotland) and came from 'burna', a once common word, evident from the number of place-names which include it: Bournemouth, Bourne End, Pangbourne, Wombourne, Lambourne, Burnham, Cranborne and many others.

There was a surprising number of words for valleys of different kinds. The general words seem to have been 'vale', 'denu' and 'dæl', from which we have obtained **Vale**, **Dean**, **Dale** and **Dell** (often though, this latter was more of a deep hollow). The word 'cumb', from which comes **Combe** was reserved for a distinctly narrow or steep sided valley. The old word 'botm' was used specifically for a valley floor, so that one whose dwelling was to be found down in the bottom of a valley may have been called **Bottom(s)**. Each of these words has its compounds: **Endean**, meaning 'duck (or lamb) valley' or simply 'valley end', **Farndell** meant 'fern hollow', **Lonsdale** implied a dweller in the valley of the River Lune (Lancashire) and **Gatcombe** was 'goat valley'.

The name which seems to cause so much embarrassment is **Bottom** (1 is listed in the London directory and 6 others on the London electoral rolls). It has a number of compounds: **Longbottom** (one living in the bottom of a long valley), **Sidebottom** (dweller on the valley side), **Rowbottom** (rough valley), **Winterbottom** (valley where the sheep and cattle were wintered) and **Higginbottom** (probably 'oaken valley'). Some bearers of such names as these are apt to feel a little self-conscious at times and have been known to adopt means of evading the feeling without quite forsaking the substance of their name. One means of escape has been to adjust the spelling. For example, **Bottom** is changed to **Botham**, which is actually very like the original sound of 'botm' (boÞm). Those who poke fun at such useful and descriptive names are usually quite unaware of their historical value and meanings. It is clearly absurd, though perhaps understandable, for those whose name is **Sidebottom**, to insist on its being pronounced 'Siddybotome' or in some similar way. Phonetic surgery has been carried out on several of the compounds by those wishing to elude the modern overtones presented by the originals, all because of the abandonment of the original meaning of the word 'bottom', a valley bottom.

Street and **Way** were obvious, if unimaginative ways in which to refer to, or locate the dwellings of folk who lived away from the village centre, although **Way** is more often found in combination with other words, giving compounds like **Greenaway**, **Holloway**, **Broadway** and **Ridgeway**, which are all self explanatory. **Lane** too, could locate a man's home and **Row(e)** was one who lived in a row of cottages. **Rhodes** and **Rodd** are both derived from the Old English word 'rodu', which meant a cleared strip of waste land allowing a rough passage – not quite a road, even though our modern word 'road' itself also derives from 'rodu'.

Descriptive names referring to various sorts of woodland have survived: **Harwood** and **Hargreaves** were woods and groves where hares were to be found and **Blackwood**, **Greenwood**, **Broadwood** and **Littlewood** gave inquirers some idea of the nature of the locality where certain peasants lived. In common with most of the surnames in this group, these too are to be found scattered across the maps of England.

The points of the compass have long featured in our names as a means of identifying the whereabouts of the dwelling of a certain member of the community. The London telephone directories reflect the general trend: **West** (868 entries), **East** (131), **North** (120) and rather a long way behind, comes **South** (77). However, **South** makes up for its poorer showing by spawning dozens of compounds, such as **Southern**, **Southfield**, **South-gate**, **Southall**, **Southwood**, **Sutton**, **Southam** ('south settlement') and so on. Most of these are of course, place-names too. The other compass points also appear in compounds: **Easton** and **Aston** (both refer to the east 'tun', a settlement) and **Eastwood**. **West** gives **Weston** (the west 'tun'), **Westwood** and **Westlake**, while **North** gives **Norton** (north 'tun'), **Norwood** and so on, often dropping its '-th-' in the process.

It was not only villagers who attracted nicknames pertaining to some nearby feature of the landscape. In the towns and cities too, we find mention of prominent features: **Wall** may have lived against the city wall or some other conspicuous wall within the town limits, while **Gates** (more often **Yates** or **Yeats** now) implied a dweller by, or keeper of one of the town entrances. **Yateman** and **Yeatman** also kept the gate. **Gates** and **Yeats** nearly always appear in their plural forms, which seems odd, until we remember that it may be possessive – 'child of Gate or Yeat'. That a town gate has given us several common surnames should not be remarkable, since towns and cities had only a limited number of gates as a simple means of controlling the passage of people through their walls and at which tolls could be collected. So, like walls, these features were important enough to have generated a surname.

Occasionally, those whose dwelling or workplace was at, or near a prominent building, acquired its name: **Lodge**, **Castle**, **Towers**, **Bridge** and **Church** (**Kirk** north of the border) are examples of this. However, there were far fewer features in the towns than in the countryside that are recalled in our surnames.

I could continue for many more pages listing and discussing the many other names which have sprung from local features of the British landscape but, having now mentioned about 150 surnames in this section and having explained the common clues to be found in prefixes and suffixes, it should be possible to work out, with some hope of success, very many other names. For instance, let's imagine we have come across the names **Addingham** and **Grisewood**. Can we dissect them to obtain their original meanings? By now, the first thing that will strike us is that they both look and sound like place-names. So, beginning with **Addingham**, we can see that it is composed of three elements:

'Add-', '-ing-' and '-ham'. Working our way backwards, we have the tell-tale suffix '-ham', which, it will be recalled, meant a village or farming settlement. The middle element '-ing-' suggests a place occupied by 'the people of ...' a leader whose personal name has, in this case, become shortened to the 'Add-' of the first syllable. Now early personal names of Old English origin often ended in '-a', so that, in our present case, we might surmise that the local leader's name may have been Adda. By this line of reasoning therefore, we have arrived at the following: **Addingham** is (or was) the name of a village that meant 'the community, or homestead, of Adda's people'. Indeed, a check in the Ordnance Survey Road Atlas of Great Britain reveals the existence of such a place about 10 miles north-west of Bradford in West Yorkshire and Professor Ekwall's Dictionary of English Place-names confirms our definition.

What, then, are we to make of the surname **Grisewood**? We can easily imagine there being a settlement of this name – it has the right look and sound. On the other hand, it could just as easily be the name describing a local wooded area. Perhaps our first move might be to check for its existence in an up-to-date road atlas. My current atlas lists no present day village of that name, so we must assume it to have been either a depopulated settlement whose site is not marked on the map, or else it was simply a local feature, a wood of some sort. Maurice Beresford, an outstanding authority on ancient deserted English villages, makes no mention of a **Grisewood** in his book 'Deserted Mediæval Villages'[1]. We can fairly assume then, that there probably was no such village. At least the suffix '-wood' is a good start, since it means what it says, but what about 'Grise-'? Ekwall's place-name dictionary[2] also does not list the name, but it does give us some clues: there are two other places beginning with 'Grise-' (and one other with 'Grize-') and each refers to pigs (from the Old Norse word 'gris', a pig). So it looks as though we would be justified in our assumption that **Grisewood** was indeed a specifically local feature, but more than that, the other three entries in Ekwall's Dictionary are in the north of England, where the Scandinavian influence was strongest (see the map on page 55). **Grisewood** must therefore, have indicated one whose dwelling was in, or near a wood where pigs were grazed and somewhere in the north of the country. The surname **Grisewood** is in fact fairly widespread throughout the country, nearly 90 being listed in electoral rolls.

Interpreting these two names was fairly straightforward, given access to standard reference books to be found on the library shelves, together with a detailed road atlas. However, there are many names that are deceptive and yet others whose meanings have become obscure

---

1. M. Beresford (1971) Deserted Mediæval Villages. Cambridge University Press.

2. E. Ekwall (1980) The Concise Oxford Dictionary Of English Place-names. Oxford University Press.

and much work has yet to be done, perhaps by enthusiastic amateurs (Dr Reaney himself, confides that his Dictionary[1] was "…begun in 1943 to beguile the quieter periods of fire-watching.") One important fact about place-names is indisputable, however – they have proved to be an enduring and invaluable record of many ancient personal names, which would have otherwise gone unrecorded and would therefore have been lost to us.

It can be entertaining to invent one's own local feature place-names; for instance, Fernby, Ravenhurst and Long Ockfield, all of which I have just made up. None of them is listed in a current road atlas or in the Dictionaries of Ekwall or Reaney, so it is not unreasonable to suppose that they may never have existed.

Let me embellish my three little fables just a little further. My imaginary hamlet of Fernby ('village in the ferns', a Danish settlement according to its '-by' suffix) lay between Lincoln and Market Rasen and was depopulated by late 1349 by the 'great pestilence', leaving no physical trace. The rare surname **Fernsby,** of which there are 3 on the London electoral registers and 5 others nationwide, may be the only remaining memory of the vanished settlement.

Continuing my fanciful invention with Ravenhurst: this is almost self-explanatory, for it meant 'the wooded hill of the ravens' and was a tiny farming community which flourished in the Yorkshire Wolds until the year 1513, when Baron Hilton, the lord of the manor, evicted the last few villagers and pulled down their cottages to extend the pasture for his increasing flocks of sheep.

Lastly, the village of Long Ockfield ('The long village with the oak-field'), between present-day Newmarket and Bury St Edmunds, suffered three consecutive drought years (1292-94). The crop failures meant that the village's remaining 16 inhabitants either perished or left the locality by night, seeking a life in Cambridge or Norwich. There is no evidence of the survival of the surname Ockfield.

Of course, all this is fantasy, but all of the events and the dates I have mentioned: the locations, the droughts, even Baron Hilton and his sheep derive from genuine records.

One could take this idea a great deal further and populate an imaginary village with inhabitants of one's own invention (having first read this book!). One would need to consider appropriate male and female personal names and a few added nicknames, as well as the tasks each of the men carried out around the village in the course of his day. Such an exercise could be very entertaining as well as instructive, especially to a youngster looking at Mediæval English life.

Although local features and occupations (discussed in Chapter Two) together account for a significant proportion (about 53%) of English

---

1. P. H. Reaney (1976) A Dictionary of British Surnames. Routledge & Keegan Paul.

surnames, two other large groups make up most of the rest: names indicating relationships and names from nicknames. Surnames derived from relationships form the second-largest surname group: about 32% of all surnames. Those from nicknames amount to roughly 12% and the remaining 3% consist of the purely personal names like **Baldwin**, **James** and **Martin**. So, in our invented village, we might include just a few of these names too.

Chapter 5

Surnames from Relationships

Using the relationship of son to father is probably the oldest established means of distinguishing one man from another. We see this clearly in the Old Testament in Chapter Five of Genesis, where the succeeding generations of **Adam** are described in terms of son to father relationships. The same is seen in Genesis Chapter Ten, where the generations of Noah's descent are revealed.

In the mediæval English village, common labourers like the ploughman, were less likely to attract an occupational nickname than those men whose office or occupation was more distinctive, like the **Reeve**, **Bailiff**, **Miller** or **Hayward**. So, how could one particular Willelm be distinguished from another Willelm living in the same village, when it came to the recording of a fine or a fee in the manorial and court records? If there was no other obvious way, such as by occupation, location or physical peculiarity, then the custom was to refer to the subject's father. Only very occasionally, however, would his mother, or some other known relative be used in the record. From surviving Saxon records we know that the genitive element '-es-' was often used, followed by the suffix '-suna' (from 'sunu', son), as in Eadric Eadmundesuna, that is Eadric, son of Eadmund. Our modern vestige of this ancient genitive case survives as -'s (that is, apostrophe 's') as in Martin's or Alfred's. In such a description as 'Eadmundesuna', it seems but a small step to the word Edmundson (there are 41 in the London telephone directory). However, we cannot overlook the intervening Latin forms used by French scriveners (scribes) after the Conquest in their attention to precision: Willelmus filius Gene[1]

---

1. P. H. Reaney (1976) *A Dictionary of British Surnames.* Routledge & Keegan Paul.

(William son of John), Alexandro filio Willelmi Saundr[1] (Alexander, son of William Saunder). In the end, it was the Saxon form that endured, so that early on we see names such as Folkesune (son of Fulk), Gibesun (son of Gibb – our eventual surname **Gibson**) and Willeson (son of Will, later emerging as **Wilson**), which were not yet hereditary in most cases. This meant, of course, that several generations of the same family could easily display a variety of descriptive names.Here is an imaginary three-generation family tree that might date from the late 11th or early 12th centuries:

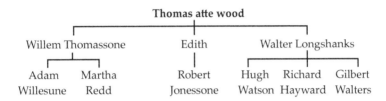

Thomas atte wood
Willem Thomassone · Edith · Walter Longshanks
Adam Willesune · Martha Redd · Robert Jonessone · Hugh Watson · Richard Hayward · Gilbert Walters

Today, all the sons, daughters, grandsons and granddaughters shown in the tree above, except for Robert Jonessone, would have the surname **Attwood**. Robert Jonessone is, of course, Edith's son, who is named after John, Edith's husband. In my example above, grandfather Thomas's nickname 'atte wood' is lost in favour of the personal names of each father. It is also noticeable that names could change according to circumstances: Walter's son, Richard, later became the village **Hayward**, a nickname of office which stuck, while Adam Willesune (that is, 'Will's son') later took a dwelling at the foot of a nearby hill and, for the villagers, he was known thereafter as Adam **Underhill**.

In the imaginary third generation of the tree, a new idea appears: instead of the three young men inheriting their father's nickname (Longshanks), or even his personal name plus the '-son' suffix (Walterson), Hugh seems to have acquired a pet form of Walter (Wat) plus '-son' (**Watson**) and Gilbert is given an abbreviated version of Walterson (**Walters**). This last name clearly means 'of Walter' here, but we have to tread carefully when faced with names ending in '-s'. We must not always assume they are genitives (that is, showing belonging), or even a short form of '-son' (see the next paragraph).

In many mediæval records, the names of married or widowed women were often set down in the following way: Cecily Willes[2], Juliana Folkes[3]. These were real people and it is known that Cecily's husband

1. P. H. Reaney (1976) *A Dictionary of British Surnames.* Routledge & Keegan Paul.

2. Ibid

3. Ibid.

was called William and that Juliana's husband was Fulk, so that the '-es' of the women's second names must imply either 'wife of' or 'widow of''. We cannot tell, therefore, what were the 'surnames' of the two husbands, unless they were recorded separately. Things are further complicated by the fact that the final '-s' in names like **Wills** and **Willis** may not be a sign of kinship at all, but signifies only an occupational connection, such as 'servant of William', or merely 'servant at the house of William'. This aspect of relationship is clearly implied in the surname **Masters**, which must mean 'at the house or workshop of the master'. The same relationship must have been indicated in many cases of **Vicars**, **Parsons** and **Monks** (but see Chapter Two for further discussion on these three names). In such cases as these we might by now expect the word 'atte' to come between the personal and second name and as we have already seen, this is often so: Gilbert atte Parsones (1332)[1] and William atte Maystres (1327)[2]. The ultimate expression of exact master-servant relationship can be seen in an entry in a 1336 roll, when one, 'William le Keu Williameservaunt Hod' is singled out[3].

Lastly, there are those occasions when the final '-s' is simply a plural, which we have already noticed in Chapter Four (Names from Local Features) in such names as **Hedges**, **Oaks** and **Waters**.

In summary then, we can see that the final '-s' of a surname can sometimes present some problems of interpretation which, at this distance in time, are often insoluble. It can imply one of five possibilities:

   (i)   'son or child, of ....';
   (ii)   'wife or widow, of ....';
   (iii)   'servant of ....';
   (iv)   'servant at ....';
   (v)   a simple plural form.

Some names have done their best to resist the encroachment of the final '-s' and have usually preferred to remain personal in their form, for example **Lawrence**, **Gilbert**, **Allan** and **Vincent**. I have located a very few **Lawrences**, **Gilberts**, **Allans** and **Vincents** in the national electoral rolls, but only in single figure numbers. Some surnames, on the other hand, have taken a middle course and are found in both forms: **Adam(s)**, **Isaac(s)**, **Matthew(s)** and **Richard(s)** are some, while at the other extreme, there are some that are rarely met today without their final '-s'. Examples of these are **Williams**, **Harris** (that is, 'of **Henry**'), **Peters**, **Roberts** and **Edwards**. The London telephone books do list examples of these names

1. P. H. Reaney (1976) *A Dictionary of British Surnames*. Routledge & Keegan Paul.

2. *Ibid.*

3. P. H. Reaney (1979 edition) *The Origin of English Surnames*. Routledge & Keegan Paul.

without their '-s' suffixes: **William** (27), **Harry** (38), **Peter** (40), **Robert** (29) and **Edward** (26), but these amount to a total of only 160 compared to many hundreds of entries of *each* of the names having the final '-s'.

Women's Names

So far, I have considered surnames that have arisen only from the personal name, sometimes called the 'font-' or 'given-' name of the father. Such names are known as 'patronymics' (Latin, 'pater', meaning father). There are, however, surnames that have their foundations in the personal name of the mother, though not so many of them. These are referred to a as 'metronymics' (Latin again, 'mater' – mother).

Before the idea of a fixed family name became common practice, the relationship to either parent was often recorded, when the need arose, by using the Latin word 'filius' (son) thus, Rogerus filius Mabilie (1130)[1] – Roger son of Mabel and Wilhelmus filius Alis (1214)[2] – William son of Alice. The use of 'filia' (daughter) is also known, but was used much more rarely.

There are several reasons which explain why a child might be called after a woman:

(i)   A child born out of wedlock might well be called after its mother;
(ii)   An adopted child, or one in the care of a female guardian;
(iii) A child brought up by its widowed mother might be known after her rather than its father;
(iv)   The child of a woman who was the dominant partner in the marriage, or whose husband was particularly feeble. There must have been some such youngsters about if the Yorkshiremen Geoffrey Liggbiyefyre ('Lie by the fire'), 1301, and Henry Lenealday ('Lean all day'), 1336, bear accurate nicknames!

Here is a list of the more popular mediæval women's names that we find increasingly recorded after the Norman Conquest and some of the surnames that have developed from them, though not all of them I have given here represent names of relationships:

Agnes	**Annis**, **Agness**;
Alice	**Alliss**, **Alison**;
Catherine	**Cattle**, **Catlin**;
Cecily	**Sissons**;

---

1. P. H. Reaney (1979 edition) *The Origin of English Surnames*. Routledge & Keegan Paul.

2. *Ibid.*

Eleanor	**Elson, Nelson**;
Mabel	**Mabbs, Mabbutt, Mobbs** and others;
Margaret	**Margetts, Margerison, Moxon, Pogson**, several others;
Mary	**Marrison, Malleson, Mallett, Mollison, Marriott** and so on;
Matilda	**Maude, Moult, Mowat, Tilson, Tillottson** and others.

Not all surnames that come from women's names date from *after* the Conquest. There is a small number of them which have their beginnings in Old English women's names of the 10th and 11th centuries. Here are some of them:

Cwenhild ('woman-war')	**Quennell**;
Godyth	**Goody**;
Leofdaeg ('love-day')	**Loveday** (a day on which personal disputes were settled);
Thurild	**Turrill**;
Tunhild	**Tunnell**.

Other Relationships

In the first part of this chapter we saw that the first and most obvious way of identifying a child was by reference to its father and occasionally, to its mother. However, other relationships were occasionally used, but they are rather rare and therefore rather interesting. In the following discussion, the numbers in brackets are the numbers of entries in the London telephone books at the time of my research, sometimes supplemented by electoral register numbers.

While **Fathers** (10) and **Mothers** (0 in London, but 49 nationwide, with a cluster in the Peterborough and Spalding districts of Lincolshire) might represent the ultimate in relationship surnames, probably the most commonly occurring name which is neither patronymic or metronymic is **Cousins** (177), which has a number of spellings. Both of these were recorded as descriptive names as early as the 10th and 11th centuries. A more frequently occurring name, though one less easy to guess is **Neave** (46) – it means 'nephew'. A rare surname nowadays is **Cister** (or **Cyster**) (9 in the London electoral lists), which may a transformation of 'sister', or it may possibly be an occupational name, referring to the maker of stone chests (Latin 'cista', a box). However, **Sisterson** (3), occurs in a few places still. **Daughters** (6) may seem an unlikely name to our eyes, but there are at least 120 recorded nationwide, 16 of them in London. There are several versions of the word **Son** (7), such as **Sonne** (6), **Sone** (7) and **Soan(es)** (26) and these nicknames may have been applied to the youngest son, in much the same way that 'junior' is used as an affectionate term today, especially in America. **Odam(s)** (6) and its variant **Odhams** (3), express the rather unexpected relationships of both brother-in-law *and* son-in-law, though, as can be seen from the London numbers, each is rare. The early English word for 'uncle' was 'eam' and this has left us with a remarkably large number of **Eames** (70), together with a few of the variant **Neame** (10). It's rather nice to note that **Uncle** (3) survives too, though only just.

In mediæval England the 'husbonda' was a man of some substance, holding both house and land, unlike the villeins and cotters and was better off than the ordinary villagers. He was likely to have been a farmer, with a wife and family living in a large house and employing a number of cotters as labourers. From this fairly modest social station we have inherited the surname **Husband(s)** (64). Later, 'husband' lost its original intimation of modest status and, as we now know, came to mean simply a married man.

As far as the relationship of **Wife** is concerned, current electoral records show that there are fewer than 30 bearers of the name, making it a possible candidate for ultimate extinction. It is the case that in manorial records, court rolls and deeds, a woman could be styled 'wyf' when the need for a specific identification was called for. Two Yorkshire examples from 1379 and 1381 will serve well to illustrate this[1]. The first woman is recorded as Joan Tomwyf, which shows that even at this time and in some places there was often no fixed surname applied to a man's wife, though in this case, we cannot tell the 'surname' of her husband (if indeed he had one); permanent surnames, as we know them, were by no means universally adopted at this time. In the second example, however, it *is* possible to learn the husband's 'surname', for the woman is recorded as Agnes Williamwyf **Smith**[2]. Here, Agnes was almost certainly the wife of William **Smith**, though she was probably not generally known as Agnes **Smith**.

If a woman was widowed, this fact was often recorded using the Latin word 'relicta' ('forsaken'), as in 'Emma relicta Johannis' (1296)[3] – that is, 'John's widow' and in 'Johanna relicta Edwardi **Jakes**' (1327)[4]. In everyday speech, the common folk would use the word 'wedue', from which comes our surname **Widdows** (8). It is interesting to notice that in the London telephone directory at the time of my research, there were twice as many **Widdowsons** (16) as there are **Widdows** (8).

One might think that the most distant point of relationship reach-

---

1. P. H. Reaney (1976) *A Dictionary of British Surnames*. Routledge & Keegan Paul.

2. P. H. Reaney (1979 edition) *The Origin of English Surnames*. Routledge & Keegan Paul.

3. *Ibid.*

4. *Ibid.*

able in names would be **Friend** (132) and **Frend** (2), but perhaps we can yet outdo even this remoteness with **Unwin,** literally 'unfriend', or more accurately, 'stranger', rather than in the sense of 'enemy'. However, some may argue that names such as these have no place in a chapter on relationships. This difference of opinion, however, is of little significance, since all surnames were originally nicknames and anyway, we are always meeting examples which fit into more than one category.

We have seen in this chapter that almost all possible relationships have been expressed and recalled in names and happily, most have survived (surprisingly so in some cases) to a greater or lesser degree, as a search through the telephone directories will reveal.

Names from the Welsh

It was not until the early 16th century that the Welsh began to adopt the English system of surnames. Until that point, they had managed with a single personal name, while only occasionally referring to 'son of …' when a more accurate identification was required. The Welsh expression for 'son of…' is 'ap' and by the reign of Henry VIII in the 15th century, some Welshmen were having to grapple with such appendages as 'Owen ap Rhys ap Madoc ap Evan'. The King pressed all Welshmen to abandon such cumbersome nomenclature and settle on a single surname after the English fashion. But national social tradition is very resistant to change, especially when imposed from outside and even today, the characteristic 'ap' is still to be found in Welsh telephone directories. The telephone book for Swansea and south-west Wales lists **ap Dewi**, **ap Gwent**, **ap Gwilym**, **ap Gwynfor**, **ap Gwynedd** and **ap Steffan**; even the London book has an **ap Simon**.

Gradually, three developments took place. Firstly, if the second name began with a letter which made pronunciation awkward when following 'ap', the 'ap' would be dropped. Thus **ap Madoc** would tend to become simply **Madoc** or **Maddock** (meaning 'good'). In 1542, King Henry VIII's 'Act Uniting England and Wales', gave further impetus to the process of change to the English surname system and we find thereafter a whole crop of Welsh names coming into regular use without their prefix 'ap': **Morgan**, a very old name, thought to mean 'sea-bright'; **Meredith**, perhaps meaning 'noble lord', or it may spring from the same source as **Morgan**. The name **Llewellyn** and its companion **Lewis**, are also problematic. Some Welsh scholars believe them to have meant 'battle-leader', while others incline to the meaning 'lion-like'. **Lewis** would also seem to have connections to the French Louis. **Lloyd** is from a word meaning 'grey' and may have referred to the colour of the bearer's hair or his ashen face. An interesting name in connection with **Lloyd** is **Blood**.

This is really a phonetic contraction of '**ap Lloyd**', son of **Lloyd**. **Trevor** meant 'grand dwelling place' and **Vaughan** comes from the Welsh word for 'little', indicating a 'pet' name or nickname. From Caradawc ('friend') we have **Craddock**. The Romans imprisoned one by the name of Caradoc and eventually sent him to Rome in AD 51, so that this name must be one of the oldest Celtic names still in use.

The second development followed the English method of showing possession: having dropped the 'ap', a final genitive '-s' was added, giving **Maddocks** (now sometimes **Maddox**), **Griffiths**, **Roberts** and **Williams**. Other familiar Welsh examples are **Davies** ('of David'), **Hughes** ('of Hugh'), **Edwards** ('of Edward') and **Jones** (from either John or Joan – both were pronounced similarly, making it impossible to determine the exact origin).

Thirdly, if the new surname began with 'H', 'R', a vowel, or sometimes 'L', the 'ap' would lose its first letter and become simply 'P-' (or the harder 'B-'). This sounds a little complicated, so a few examples should clarify things. **Ap Owen** became **Bowen**, **ap Howell** became **Powell**, **ap Evan** became **Bevan** and **ap Richard** became **Pritchard** (which has somehow acquired an unnecessary and intrusive '-t-' in the middle). Others in this Welsh group are **Pugh** (**ap Huw**), **Pumphrey** (**ap Humphrey**), **Preece** and **Price** (**ap Rhys**), **Barry** and **Parry** (both **ap Harry**). The surname **Upjohn** is an odd case, being **ap John**, while **Upritchard** (pronounced 'yu-Pritchard') seems an even more curious throwback. We can see all three developments individually in the surnames **Owen**, **Owens** and **Bowen** and all three at once in **Proberts**.

A few names refer to Welsh places. The ones most likely to be encountered are **Prendergast** (in Dyfed) and **Conway** (in Gwynedd). **Cardiff** (the city), **Clwyd** (a county in north-west Wales) and **Flint** (a town in the county of Clwyd) are occasionally to be found too. There are others, though they will be seen in fairly small numbers.

It seems then, that Welsh surnames are historically mostly of one type: that which recalls the father-son relationship.

Names from Scotland

If Welsh surnames seemed to be without much variety in their system, we shall find rather more diversity in those from Scotland. Apart from the expected set of surnames paying homage to the kings of that country, there are many toponymics (that is, names from places or local features). Firstly, the kings' names: **Malcolm** ('follower of St Columba'), **Duncan** (Old Gaelic 'brown-warrior'), **Alexander** ('defender of men') and **James**, which have also produced a small crop of patronymics: **Sanderson** ('Alexander's son') and **Jameson** for instance. The toponymics include

Burn(s) and **Beck** (both meaning 'stream' and are equivalent to the English **Brook(s)**), **Kirk** (equal to **Church**) and so forth. However, in the Lowlands, once a part of the Anglo-Saxon kingdom of Northumbria, the impact of English-type names was strong, as we should expect and there is a great similarity between the names of relationship in the two regions, the suffix '-son' being as widely applied as it was in England. Further north, in the Highlands, where Gaelic was the natural language, we find a different system of naming based on clan or family loyalty. In this method, the personal name of the clan leader was prefixed by 'Mc-' ('son of …'), which soon came to imply 'descendant of …' and even 'follower of …' as the kinship and clan loyalty factors became powerful binding forces in tribal structure.

'Mc-' and 'Mac-' tended to appear in front of not only typically Scottish personal names: **McGregor** ('of **Gregory**'), **McLauren** ('of **Laurence**'), **McTavish** ('of **Thomas**'), but in front of common English names too. Examples of this are **McAdam**, **McMichael** and **McWilliam**. Even essentially Welsh personal names have not escaped: **McIvor**, **McOwen** and **McHugh** occur in small numbers.

A few names have arisen through the nicknaming process. Unlike the English, who nicknamed each other freely, the Scots sometimes applied their leaders' names to the clans that they led. Two well-known ones are **Cameron** ('crooked nose') and **Campbell** ('crooked mouth'). From their relatively remote homelands, these clan names have become dispersed across the face of the globe in a remarkably short time. So, to end this section, I will list twenty familiar Scottish surnames, all of which mean, of course, 'son of …', 'descendant of …' or 'follower of …' the clan leader whose name is given:

McAlister	– Alexander;
McCallum	– St Columba;
McCartney	– Arthur;
McCaskill	– Askell;
McDonald	– Donald;
McDougal	– Dougal (from Dhubgall);
McFadden	– Patrick;
McHendrie	– Henry;
McInnes	– Angus;
McIntosh	– 'Son of the Chieftain';
McKay	– 'Son of Aoh';
McKellar	– Hillary;
McKim	– **Simon**;
McLean	– Ian (that is, **John**);
McLeod	– 'Son of the ugly one';
McMillan	– 'Son of the bald one';

McNicol	– Nicholas;
McPherson	– 'Son of the Parson';
McRae	– 'Son of grace';
McTaggart	– 'Son of the priest'.

Irish Surnames

'Mc-', or 'Mac-', may also be a sign of relationship in Irish history in a similar way to its role in the Scottish Gaelic. Again the prefix is followed by a personal name, often with a change of spelling from the original Gaelic form in order to make it more easily pronounceable to the English; for example, **McKenna** means 'of Cionaodh' and **McGowan** means 'of ghobhainn' (that is, a smith).

There was so much movement of people between Ireland and Scotland before and during the middle ages, that it is not always possible to distinguish names of Scottish origin from the purely Irish ones. **Macaulay** is a case in point: its Irish meaning is 'son of Amalghaidh', but the Hebridean meaning is 'relic of the gods'.

Most people will be aware that surnames prefaced with 'O'-' are of Irish origin and that such names show possession or descent: **O'Connor** (Conchobhair, 'descendant of one called 'high will'') and **O'Brien** (Briain, 'of one who dwelt on a hill', 'high' or 'noble') are familiar examples. Other typically descriptive Irish names are **Kennedy** (Cinnéide, 'ugly head'), **Murphy** (Murchadha, 'sea-warrior') and **Milligan** ('little bald head'), **Kelly** (Ceallaigh – 'bright-headed'), **Regan** (Riagáin, 'little king'), **Lynch** (Loinsigh, 'sea-farer', 'exile'), **Sheehan** (Siodhachain, 'peaceful') and **Brennan** (Braonáin, 'sorrowful one').

King Henry VII showed some concern about the Welsh system of naming and I have already referred to the encouragement given to the Welsh to simplify their naming system, by his son Henry VIII, in his 1542 Act of Unification. It seems likely, however, that these two monarchs were prompted in their actions by the example of King Edward IV, whose law of 1465 instructed every Irishman to take a surname after the English manner, that is, to adopt a place-name, an occupational name or a nickname and thereafter to cause it to be inherited by his children. No mention was made of names showing relationship, because these had been in use since the 11th century, by the addition of 'O'-'to an ancestor's personal name. One of King Edward's reasons for pursuing this line undoubtedly included the standardisation of surnames in Ireland in common with those in England, thus binding the two peoples closer together, as well as removing the complications arising from the spellings and pronunciation of Irish names – awkward for Englishmen. One is left wondering, however, whether the resentment that such laws must have generated among the native Irish, might have out-weighed the advantages the king thought he foresaw in such a scheme.

Like the Scottish Mc-s, the Irish Mc-s and O'-s have spread far and wide, especially to the New World of course.

So, to end our look at Irish names, I will list some of the names of the Irish together with their meanings, as I did with those of the Scots. Here they are:

McCafferty (Eachmharcaig)	'..... of the steed-rider';
McCann (Cana)	'.... of the wolfhound';
McCusker (Oscair)	'.... of Oscar', or 'of the champion';
McElroy (Giolla Ruaidh)	'.... of the red-haired one';
McGee (Aoidh)	'.... of Aodh' (fire);
McGuire (Uidhir)	'.... of the dun-coloured one';
MacManus (Haghnuis)	'.... of Magnus' (Latin 'great');
MacNamara (Conmara)	'.... of the sea-hound';
McKenna (Cionaoith)	'.... fire-sprung';
MacDermott (Diarmada)	'.... free from jealousy';
McCarthy (Carthaig)	'.... of the loving person';
McTigue (Teague)	'.... of the poet';
O'Connell (Conaill)	'.... strong as a wolf';
O'Donnell (Domhnaill)	'.... world-mighty';
O'Farrell (Fearghail)	'.... of the man of valour';
O'Hare (Hehir)	'.... of the angry one';
O'Keefe (Caoimh)	'.... of the tender one';
O'Leary (Laoghaire)	'.... of the calf-keeper';
O'Neil (Néill)	'.... of the champion';
O'Shea (Séaghdha)	'.... of the stately one';
O'Toole (Tuathail)	'.... of 'people-mighty'.

A Norman Postscript

After the Conquest, the Normans introduced the term 'le fils', meaning 'the son', when recording names in documents. English tongues soon corrupted this to 'le fiz' and it began to make its appearance in records thus, 'Reginald le fiz' or 'Robert Fiz'. Before long, it had become a prefix in its own right: 'Fitz-' and a number of personal names found themselves sounding a shade more distinguished: **FitzAlan**, **FitzGibbon**, **FitzGilbert**, **FitzMaurice**, **FitzSimmonds**, **FitzWalter** and **FitzWilliam** are some of them.

Chapter 6

Surnames from Words of Affection

For some time before each of us was born, our parents must have given a good deal of thought and much discussion to the name they would choose for the new member of the family. They finally chose a name which they found most appealing or appropriate, just as parents have always done. Often in the past, a child would be named after a parent or grandparent, perhaps out of respect or in particular memory of the chosen adult. Sometimes a distinguished personage – the king or queen, a statesman or a well-known or admired individual – would be the inspiration for the name. The 'given' name would then be formally registered on the child's birth certificate as proof of identity. Many parents, however, realise that things can happen to a child's name when other children get to work on it, especially at school, where it can be instantly transformed into something unflattering and quite unanticipated. These parents are careful then, to take this into account when making their choice. Nevertheless, transformations of names at the hands of one's fellows have always happened and the English have been (and still are) very lively inventors in this respect. Today's Robert is likely to be called Rob, Robbie, Bob or Bobby by parents and friends, except on formal occasions, though even here, the former starchiness is often lightened nowadays by the increasing use of more friendly means of address, perhaps encouraged by the perceived American liking for an immediate contact on a familiar level. Thus 'pet' forms of names are frequently to be found where, in bygone times, only the unadulterated personal name would have been acceptable.

In the 13th century, Robert was often shortened to Rob, Dob, Hob and occasionally Nob: these four alone giving rise to several dozen subsequent surnames. Here are some of our surnames whose origins lie in those four 'pet' names: **Robbs, Robbins, Robinson, Rabbs, Rabson, Dobbs, Dobson, Hobbs, Hobson, Hopkins, Hopkinson, Nobbs** and **Noblett**. There are also several variations on the original Robert too, most of which will be quite familiar to us.

Englishmen had a curious and characteristic taste for shortening names to a single syllable – usually the first – and then further getting to work on that, as we have just seen in the examples based on Robert. We can see this process at work on other popular personal names of post-Conquest centuries. Here are some surname variations on eight familiar male personal names:

David	– **Dawes, Dawson, Dawkins, Davy, Davis, Davison, Day**;
Herbert	– **Harbard, Harbutt, Herbison, Hibbs, Hipkiss**;
Nicholas	– **Nichols, Nix, Nixon, Colls, Collins, Collett, Coull, Coulson**;
Richard	– **Rich, Ricketts, Rix, Hicks, Hickson, Higgins, Hitchen, Dicks, Dix, Diggins, Dickens**;
Roger	– **Dodge, Dodgson, Dodson, Hodge, Hodgson, Hodgkinson, Hadgkiss**;
Thomas	– **Tomms, Tombs, Tomlin, Tamblin, Tomkins, Tompkins, Tomkinson**;
Walter	– **Watt, Watts, Wattis, Watkins, Watson, Watkiss**;
William	– **Wills, Willis, Wilson, Wilmot, Willett, Wilcock**.

These names show the whimsy possible when the 13th century lower classes were given so many imported Norman French names to play with. Not all newly introduced names were of Norman origin, however, for some had German roots. The Norman conquerors were, nevertheless, responsible for their proliferation on this side of the English Channel.

Women's names could not escape the diminutive process and transformation, any more than could those of the men and the boys and I listed some of their variations in Chapter Five (Surnames from Relationships). Here are three others which are interesting in that they illustrate how far a 'pet' name can get from its parent form:

Beatrice	– **Beatty, Beeton**;
Emma	– **Emms, Emmett, Empson**;
Isabel	– **Ibbottson, Tibbs, Libby, Bibby**.

The eventual spelling of many names began to reflect the differences in regional pronunciation. One important change was the result of the way in which some districts softened some sounds. Here are some examples of the effects of this softening process:

Dennison becomes **Tennyson** ('son of Denis') in which the 'T' is a softened or unvoiced 'D';

Dyson becomes **Tyson** in some places ('son of Dye') – again, with a softened 'D';

Hib- becomes Hip- in **Hipkiss** ('little Heb', a pet name for **Herbert**). The 'p'
    sound is the unvoiced 'b';
Hob- becomes Hop- in **Hopkins** ('little Hob', Robert);
Hodgkins becomes **Hotchkins** ('little Hodge', Roger);
(Words ending in -kin, -kins and -kiss are discussed a little later in this chapter).

In some districts, instead of a softening of the sounds (that is, from
voiced to unvoiced forms), the reverse occurred – a distinct hardening
took place:

Foss became **Voss** ('dweller by the ditch', Latin 'fossa', a ditch);
Fiddler became **Vidler** or **Viddler** ('player of the fiddle');
Dicks became **Digges** ('of Richard'), the soft '-ck-' became the hard '-gg-'.

Changes of spelling sometimes arose early on because clerks, who
were mostly Norman at first, would simply record the same unfamiliar
Old English sounds in different ways, which easily explains the alternative spellings of the same names that are found side by side. There
are several common instances of these which have persisted through
many centuries: the '-x' instead of the more obviously genitive '-cks'
in names like **Cox**, **Wix** and **Hixon**, rather than **Cocks**, **Wicks** and
Hickson (which are also found today of course). The letters '-i-' and '-y-'
became interchangeable in some names: **Pile** and **Pyle** and **White** and
Whyte are examples of such caprice, while 'Ph-' sometimes takes the
place of the letter 'F' in surnames like **Filby** (and **Philby**) and **Jeffcott**
(and **Jephcott**). Doubling of central letters is also found: **Denison** and
Dennison, **Crosland** and **Crossland**. There are so many other cases of
variations of spelling that many pages could be devoted to their listings
and discussion. However, such cases do have a bearing on our consideration of names that show affection and friendliness, because some of these
changes were the results of the formation and adoption of 'pet' names.
Today, we will often add a '-y' or '-ie' (less often, an '-o') to the shortened personal name. Even so, Joey, Vicky, Debbie and Bobbo remain
purely 'pet' names and have probably made no impression on surname
formation, because they arose after the surname-forming period. They
all suggest the friendly and affectionate idea of 'little' and have a flavour
of fondness about them: Mandy is only a way of saying 'Little Amanda',
Jackie is 'Little Jack or Jacqueline', while Tommy and Tommo are of
course 'Little Tom'.
    We might well wonder whether 'pet' suffixes were added by parents
or friends to the personal names of mediæval children. The answer is
– yes, they were. The two 'pet' suffixes most often used were '-kin' and
'-cock'. The earlier of the two forms was '-kin' and began to appear in the
early 12th century in Flanders or thereabouts. The other suffix, '-cock',

however, may be home-grown and there is at least a dozen explanations for the suffix '-cock' appearing in surnames. Here I list the most important of them:

1. Sometimes '-cock' was confused in ordinary speech and dialect with '-cott';
2. Inn-keepers were sometimes called after the sign of the inn which they kept;
3. The Old English word 'cocc' meant a mound or hillock. This may have been a local feature near to which a man had his dwelling; 'Thomas attecok (1380)[1], ' by the hill';
4. There is evidence[2] that Koc was a personal name, which accounts for 'Koc filius Pertuin (1296), that is Koc, son of Pertuin;
5. The Old English word for a cook was 'coc'. Clerks and scribes often co nfused 'cock' and 'cook';
6. Sometimes it comes directly from the name of a bird: **Peacock** and **Woodcock**, for example;
7. At times, the suffix '-cock' was added to the name of the child's father to imply 'son of', as in Richard Dobcock ('Richard, son of Dob' , a pet name for Robert);
8. It was also a word often applied to a boy who was pert and lively and who possessed a cock-like impishness – 'cocky' as he might be called today.

We need not bother here about the ones listed from 1 to 5. Number 6 amounts to a nickname and Nicknames have a chapter to themselves (Chapter Seven), while number 7 is a means of denoting relationship, which I have already discussed in Chapter Five. This leaves us with its use as a 'pet' suffix (number 8 above).

We can easily imagine Adam, a lively young rascal, being called **Adcock** by his father and mother, or little Richard earning the nickname **Hitchcock** for his sauciness. There are very many instances of the shortened personal name to which has been added '-cock'. Most are the personal names of boys. Soon, however, some of these names acquired a possessive '-s', which sometimes became transformed into an '-x', as I previously mentioned, rather disguising the real meaning of the word: **Wilcox** ('of little William'), **Hancox** ('of little Hann', a 13th century form of **John**) and **Hitchcox** ('of little Richard').

The suffix '-kin' and its close relatives '-kins' and '-kiss' are also commonly seen. They too, were a means of expressing fondness and were also appended to the shortened personal or 'pet' name. We still

---

1. P. H. Reaney (1979 edition) *The Origin of English Surnames*. Routledge & Keegan Paul.

2. E. Weekley (1936) *Surnames*. Murray.

occasionally use the '-kins' version in this affectionate way, when playfully addressing a favourite person: 'Daddykins' and 'Babykins' for example. We usually find that the '-kins' form is rather more frequent that '-kin'. This may have arisen from the 'belonging to' genitive in some instances or it may reflect the peculiar English practice of smoothing out an otherwise slightly abrupt ending, as we sometimes hear today in Cockney areas: "'Allo ducks", rather than "'Allo duck" and 'muggins' instead of 'muggin' (a simpleton). Indeed, the final '-s' in such cases has almost acquired the status of a 'pet' suffix on its own account.

In some cases the shortening of the personal name has been so extreme that it is a puzzle to identify its original form. What do you make of **Larkin**? You'll now recognise that the '-kin' implies an affectionate 'little', but how about the diminutive 'Lar-': what can this be short for? What personal name could possibly be shortened to 'Lar'? In fact, Lar (and Lor) are abbreviated forms of **Laurence** and **Lawrence**, so that **Larkin** is 'little Laurence'.

Here are some more of these very short or transformed 'pet' names, to which the suffixes '-kin' or '-kins' were added:

Adkin, Aitkin	– 'Little **Adam**';
Alkin, Alchin	– 'Little **Alan** or **Alexander**';
Pipkin	– 'Little Philip'. **Filkins**, 'child of Little Philip', or one from the Oxfordshire village of Filkins;
Hankin	– 'Little Hann', that is, John;
Halkin	– 'Little Hal', that is **Henry**;
Hawkins	– 'of little **Henry**';
Hinkin, Henkin	– 'Little **Henry**' or 'little Hann' (**John**);
Hipkins	– 'Little Heb', that is **Herbert**;
Makin, Meakin	– 'Little **Matthew**' (also found as **Mathew** and **Mayhew**);
Malkin	– 'Little Mal', that is Mary;
Parkin	– 'Little Peter';
Perkins	– 'child of Little Peter';
Rankin	– 'Little Ran', that is Ranulf (a personal name that has, regrettably, all but disappeared).

In **Tompkins** ('of little Thomas') and **Simpkin** ('little **Simon**'), we again see the typically English liking for the smoothing process between one syllable and the next, by inserting an almost, but not quite, silent '-p-' between them. It also occurs in **Thompson, Sampson, Simpson, Bampford, Hampson** and **Hampton**, each of which is also found without the intrusive letter. Its intrusion seems to require a preceding '-m-' sound and a succeeding particular consonant such as '-f-', '-s-' and '-t-'.

It's worth noticing that many of the '-kins' adopted the alternative suffix '-kiss', as in **Perkiss, Hipkiss, Watkiss** and **Hadgkiss**. This may have come about as much through regional peculiarities of speech as through the 'smoothing' process. Just when this particular variation began to appear is difficult to say. However, one Shropshire record mentions a John **Hotchkiss** ('little Roger')[1] in the year 1690, which suggests it may be a late development.

So much then, for these two important suffixes. Other suffixes were imported from Normandy after the Conquest and soon established themselves. These include '-el', '-ell', '-in', '-on', '-ett', '-ot' and '-ott', each of which served to express a similar affection or fondness to '-cock' and '-kin'. Again, we have to resort to using the affectionate word 'little' when trying to put a meaning to the names.

Here are some familiar appearances of these endings:

Dickin, **Dicken**	– 'little Richard';
Gibbon	– 'little Gibb' (that is, **Gilbert**);
Hewell	– 'little Hugh';
Luckett	– 'little Luke';
Wilmot, **Willett**	– 'little **William**'.

Sometimes we come across two at once: a double diminutive:

Bartlett	– Bart(holomew) + '-el-' + '-ett';
Hewlett	– Hew (Hugh) + '-el-' + '-ett';
Tomlin, **Tambling**	– **Thomas** + '-el-' + '-in-'.

In the surname Tambling, mentioned above, we see again the sliding effect obtained by the intrusive '-b-'. It is interesting to discover that the original spellings of **Bartlett** and **Tomlin** were **Bartelot** and **Tomelyn**, subsequent usage having modified them. Nevertheless, the idea of a double diminutive does seem a little capricious, if not eccentric, especially when we try to express a literal definition – 'little, little....'!

Others in this curious group are:

Hewlin	– Hew (Hugh) + '-el-' + '-in';
Parnell	– Peter + '-in-' + '-ell';
Rawlins	– Ralf + '-el-' + '-ins' ('of little Ralf');
Roblett	– Robert + '-el-' + '-ett'.

Is it clear to us by now, that the scope for forming such 'pet' or affectionate diminutives of personal names in the 12th-14th centuries must have been enormous and due, to a very large extent, to the infusion of the Norman suffixes.

---

1. P. H. Reaney (1979 edition) *The Origin of English Surnames*. Routledge & Keegan Paul.

I thought I would bring this chapter on affectionate names to a close by looking at the huge number of variations that are to be found on two common personal names, Robert and Margaret.

Robert was always a popular name and derived from the Old English name Hreodbeorht ('fame-bright') and was much loved by the Normans:

Robert, Roberts, Robards, Robarts, Robb, Robbs, Robbens, Robbins,
Robbie, Roby, Robey, Robbies, Robblett, Roberson, Robertson, Robeson,
Robin, Robins, Robinson, Robjohn, Robjohns, Roblett, Roblin, Robson,
Rabbatts, Rabbitt, Rabbitts, Rabjohn, Rabjohns, Rabson, Rablin;
Dobb, Dobbs, Dobberson, Dobbin, Dobbins, Dobbing, Dobie, Dobinson,
Dobison, Dobson, Dobbyn, Dabb, Dabbs, Dabson;
Hobb, Hobbs, Hobbins, Hobby, Hoblyn, Hobson, Hopson, Hobgen,
Hopkin, Hopkins, Hopkinson;
Nobbs, Noblett, Nabbs, Napp, Napps, Nappin;
Probert, Probet, Probets, Probitts, Probyn.

That so many variations (there are 67 listed above) on a single personal name are possible is astonishing (and there may be a few more than I have listed). It is also amazing how far from the original Robert it is possible to get – **Nappin** has no letters in common with the original word! This list reflects not only the popularity of the name Robert, but also the inventiveness of the mediæval English domestic mind. Twenty-four of the names in the list show the diminutive elements we have been looking at in this chapter and these variations are by no means all that are known to exist on this name. Indeed, if this exercise were repeated with the six most popular mediæval boys' names, we should find there were several hundred variations still in use today.

Next, those names that have Margaret as their foundation. It too, has been a well-used and favourite name, especially in Scotland, though south of the border its popularity waned rapidly in the latter half of the 20th century. The name comes from the Greek word *margaron*, 'a pearl'. Here are the majority of its variations:

Margrett, Margetts, Margetson, Margey, Margrie, Margery;
Margerison, Margerrison, Margesson;
Magg, Maggs, Magson, Madgett, Madge;
Megg, Meggs, Meggitt, Megson;
Mogg, Moxon;
Pegg, Peggs, Pegges, Peggie;
Pogson.

There are 25 variations on the surname Margaret listed above, but again, these are not all of the known permutations. However, there are far fewer surviving surnames deriving from girls' personal names than from those of boys. The ones from girls which give the greatest number of variations are Mary, Margaret, Isabel, Matilda and Mabel

Here we must leave 'pet' names and names showing affection and move on to those surnames that we think of as being nicknames in the more familiar sense of the word.

Chapter 7

Nicknames

What are Nicknames?

The word 'nickname' is the result of an elision, that is, words that are run together in speech – in this case the words are 'an eke name'. Chambers Dictionary defines 'eke' thus: 'to add to, increase; to lengthen, supplement'. This last is exactly what a nickname amounted to, an extra name which was added to the personal name. We create nicknames without thinking much about what we are doing, when we say something like, "There's young Tom", or "There goes old Mary". We are affectionately identifying two people by using their respective ages as a means of popular recognition and we may, at the same time, simply be distinguishing Tom and Mary from others of the same names. By singling out a remarkable feature, we are continuing a practice that has been going on for many centuries. These nicknames often stick and Tom may be called 'Young Tom' even when he has grown up.

As a small boy, I remember a neighbouring family in which both father and son were called Arthur. The son was always referred to as 'Little Arthur', even after he had grown into a strapping young man, while his father was 'Big Arthur' even into old age. A man who also lived close by, was known as 'Sailor Jack', on account of his sea-faring background. I'm sure most people can recall similar examples from their own lives and localities. This sort of simple nicknaming process has gone on for many generations of course, and will continue to do so, in private, at least. Every school is a rich fountain of nicknames; some are simple and short, some are artful and witty, others are downright mischievous, but all show that particular English fondness for invention. It is useless deploring some of the names we overhear today, since our ancestors were lively and cutting in their own descriptions of their fellows. When investigating ancient records, we encounter a huge variety of nicknames

– some unutterably coarse to our minds.

The following exchange between two East Londoners, is based on a quotation by the scholar Ernest Weekley in his study of surnames[1] and well illustrates the lengths possible when folk get going:

> "'Ere Ginger, who was that bit o' skirt what I see yer wiv last night?"
> "What, the bird wiv the 'air-do?"
> "Naa, 'er wiv the legs."
> "Oh, Moanin' Mavis yer mean. That's the governor's bit of 'omework really, so keep yer trap shut Lofty, will yer?"

In this short passage there are four actual (and obvious) nicknames – Ginger, Moanin' Mavis, Lofty and the governor – and six hidden expressions which amount to nicknames – 'bit o' skirt', 'bird wiv the 'air-do', ''er wiv the legs', 'that', 'bit of 'omework' and 'trap'.

The group of surnames which has its origins in ancient nicknames, is vast and in spite of the disappearance of a large proportion of such names, we shall see that an enormous number remains and in tremendous variety. In some respects, this group is the most interesting of the four categories of surnames, since it gives us a valuable glimpse into some of the thinking processes of our ancestors, at their tastes and into the nature of their wit. Of course, all surnames began as nicknames in the sense that they were descriptions appended to individuals' personal names, as a means of characterisation.

Our resourceful ancestors would confer a nickname, having first perceived some singular feature about the individual in question. The sorts of things that would have been likely to draw comment are the following:

(i)   Appearance;
(ii)   Temperament and character;
(iii)   Behaviour;
(iv)   Dress;
(v)   Performing ability (music, acting, dancing, pageants etc);
(vi)   The time or season of birth;
(vii)   An entirely abstract idea.

Nicknames from physical appearance

In his book 'Britannia', first published in 1586 and running through six editions by 1607, William Camden tells us that the Romans had names for those unfortunate enough to be born with blemishes, deformities and

---

1. E. Weekley (1936) *Surnames*. Murray.

other imperfections. Translated from the Latin, we have the following instances:

Fronto ('Beetlebrow' – one having heavy eyebrows, probably);
Nasica or Silanus ('Bottlenose', an unusually large nose or perhaps one that dripped copiously);
Flaccus ('Flag-ears', prominent, large ears no doubt);
Vermis ('Maggot' – we can only wonder about this individual);
Calvus, ('Baldpate' an unusually bald head);
Cincinnatus ('Curly-haired', unusually crinkled hair for a Roman, perhaps);
Vatia ('Knock-kneed' – seems to speak for itself!);
Scaeva ('Left-handed', a peculiarity clearly worth comment);
Strabo and Paetus ('Squint', probably cross-eyed).

If the Romans were plain speakers when it came to describing each other, the mediæval peasants were no less so and pulled no punches when labelling their fellows. Fortunately perhaps, almost all of the coarser nicknames quickly disappeared with the deaths of their bearers, leaving a legacy of less objectionable epithets for future generations to work on.

We have inherited a large number of surnames derived from nicknames relating to the human form and it may be interesting to begin by looking at some opposites.

Long (**Lang** and **Laing** in Scotland), together with variations like **Longman**, **Longfellow**, **Lank**, **Lankey**, **Langson** and **Tall** all record someone in the neighbourhood of unusual height. An interesting entry in one telephone directory I consulted was **Longmaid**: an unusually tall woman would certainly draw forth comment in a small community. **Longmate** is a variation on **Longmaid**.

At the other extreme, **Short**, **Shorter**, **Shortman**, **Lesser**, **Bass**, **Bassett**, **Court** (that is 'curt') and **Courtauld** all refer to smallness of stature. **Shorthouse** is a corruption of 'short-hose', however and alludes to 'short legs' or even a 'short neck'. Similarly, **Little**, **Littleboy**, **Littlechild**, **Littler**, **Littlejohn**, **Small** and **Smale** all mean what they say. Less obvious, however, are **Lilleyman** and **Lutman**. These are both transformations of **Littleman**.

If unusual stature attracted nicknames, then so did exceptional girth of body, producing such names as **Bigg**, **Biggerman**, **Gross**, **Broad**, **Broadribb**, **Round** and **Thick(e)**, amongst others. Names of similar meaning are **Stout**, **Grant** (that is, 'grand'), while from Scotland we have **Mickle**, **Meikle** and **Micklejohn** ('big John').

Mayne and **Maynard** originate in Old German and once recalled exceptional strength rather than great size. At the other end of the scale, **Thinne** and **Meager** (each with two or three variants), **Lean** and **Slim**

might draw forth a sneer today if their bearers' physiques were out of keeping with their surnames. This reminds us that there has always been a waggish inclination on the part of Englishmen to confer a nickname exactly the opposite of the real description. 'Tiny' applied to a tall or large person and 'Lofty' to a small one, are not usually felt to be offensive, though it is unlikely that we would come across a 'Fatty' or a 'Skinny', even given in irony, since modern sensibilities are encouraged to be delicate and are easily bruised by remarks about what is always regarded, in the western world at any rate, as an undesirable and unmentionable physical flaw. Children though, are likely to be cuttingly exact, especially in anger, until they learn to apply discipline and tact to their tongues. Our mediæval ancestors, however, would have had no hesitation in applying such accurate (or ironical) descriptions to each other.

The Head and Face

Nicknames applied to the head most often referred to its size or shape, though hair colour could give rise to a name too, as in **Blackett** ('black head or hair'). **Head** itself, is not an uncommon name (there are 24 listed in my local 'phone book) and **Greathead** appears in most directories, as does **Broadhead**. The original bearers of these nicknames must have had heads worthy of comment. In many cases, the suffix '-head' has been reduced to '-ett', as is characteristic of the English economy of pronunciation and so we find examples of **Smollett** ('small head'), **Parrett** ('pear-shaped head'), **Doggett** ('dog head') and **Bullett** ('bull head'). There are some other names of this type that we shall meet when we consider nicknames in other groups. However, just to introduce a little confusion, we must remember that the suffix '-ett' has another important meaning. As we saw in Chapter Six (Surnames from Words of Affection), it was introduced by the Normans as a diminutive and a sign of endearment, which we interpret as 'little'. Thus **Duckett** does not mean 'duck head', but 'Little Marmaduke'!

The face probably produced many more nicknames than we now use, or even know about, though not many of them found their way into written records and those that were put down are mostly obsolete now. However, four of them are worth a mention. By far the most common are **Beck** and **Beckett**, though both of these names have alternative origins. **Beck** is sometimes a variation of 'beak' and referred to a prominent beak-like nose, while **Beckett** contains the common Norman diminutive suffix '-ett' and can mean 'little sharp nose'. An Old English name for the snout was 'wrot' and it is from this word that we have the interesting, but rare surname **Wroot**, of which there are 4 entries in the London registers of electors and 198 countrywide. Nicknames known to have been applied to mediæval bearers of impressive noses were Langnase ('long nose'), Kattisnese ('cat's nose') and Oxenose ('ox-nose')[1]. All of these are now, mercifully, long since extinct, descriptive though they are.

The remaining feature of facial structure to have stood the test of time is **Cheek**, a nickname usually given to one with a prominent jaw. The complexion and its crop of nicknames will be discussed in the section on the next page.

The eyes can be the most striking feature of a face and colour names with the suffix '-ie' nearly always indicate the nature of the eyes. **Blackie** ('black eye') given to someone with uncommonly dark eyes, **Brownie** ('brown eye') and **Goldie** ('gold eye') occur in small numbers, while the rare name **Bridie**, with its transposed second and third letters, meant 'bird eye'. To these names we should add a few ending in '-y' and '-ey', though here too, we must make no assumptions: '-ey' is a common representation of the Old Norse word for an island, to be found in such names as **Osney** ('Osa's island'), **Coney** ('rabbit island'), **Whitney** ('white island') and **Sheppey** ('sheep island'). **Birdy** ('bird eye') is a commoner version of **Bridie**. **Brady** and **Brodie** meant 'broad eye' and probably referred to widely spaced eyes. **Smalley** was either 'small eye' or from small-ley, that is, 'small-wood'. **Smellie** and **Smillie** both recalled one with small eyes. **Goosey**, perhaps predictably, could be 'goose eye', or might refer to one whose home was on, or near, the island of the geese.

The occasional cleft lip is remembered in the nickname **Cudlipp** ('cut lip').

The Hair and Complexion

Although almost every colour is represented in our surnames, not every instance has its origins in the appearance of hair or complexion, for there must have been some occasions when the dyer or purveyor of coloured cloths was nicknamed after one of the colours he supplied, while the man who habitually wore a particular colour might also have acquired a colour nickname. Probably the least frequently encountered colour is yellow, with only one entry of **Yellowe** in the London 'phone book, together with 4 others on the London electoral registers. It is a very rare name today: checking the national electoral archive reveals only 11 holders of this name. In mediæval times, yellow was a colour associated particularly with the Jews in the towns, who would often wear distinctive yellow caps or hoods and this may be a source of the name worth considering. The few examples of **Jellow** and **Jallow** still to be found, are unlikely to be echoes of the colour yellow, but are probably

---

1. P. H. Reaney (1979 edition) *The Origin of English Surnames*. Routledge & Keegan Paul.

derived from the Middle English word 'jalous' meaning 'jealous'. Yellow is also fairly rare in its compounds: **Yellowley** and **Yellowlees** (317 recorded nationally), each of which signifies one who must have had some connection with a clearing or meadow in which a profusion of yellow flowers or perhaps well-ripened corn could be seen. Yellowish coloured hair was not uncommon, but it was usually referred to as 'golden' – hence **Goulden** and is one origin of **Gould** and **Gold**. From the Latin 'flavus' we have the surname **Flavell**, which, in all likelihood, alluded to the yellowish colour of the subject's hair and may be a diminutive (note the characteristic Norman '-ell' suffix).

Another unusual name in the colour group, though one which I have personally encountered in Oxford, is **Purple**. This nickname may have been gained by a man (or even a woman) whose complexion had a purplish hue, or else it may have been the nickname of a dyer, a seller or wearer of purple cloth. The same explanations must also apply to the original bearers of the nickname **Scarlett**.

The more familiar colours and some of their compounds are listed below:

Red	– **Redd, Rudd, Read, Reade, Reid** (though these last three have alternative origins), **Redhead, Redman, Russell, Rouse**;
Brown	– **Brown, Browne, Broun, Broune, Bruin, Bron**;
Black	– **Black, Blake, Blackman, Blakelock** ('black locks');
Grey	– **Gray, Grey, Grice, LeGrys**;
White	– **White, Whyte, Whitehead, Whitman, Whitlock** ('white locks').

Blue, though known as an uncommon surname, may have suggested a dyer or seller of that colour cloth. Alternatively, a child with intensely blue eyes may have earned the nickname. It may, as some scholars believe, have one of its origins in the name **Blow**, a nickname for a blower of horns. Eye colour may well be the explanation of the two surnames **Bluett** and **Blewett**, the French diminutive '-ett' signifying that here we probably have no more than a charmingly affectionate 'little blue-eyes'.

One of our most abundant and familiar colour-surnames is **Green** but, of all the colours, this one is most out of place in this section, for it had no connection whatever with complexion, skin, hair or eyes – how could it?. It was in fact, no more than a nickname acquired by one whose dwelling was hard by the village green, as is evidenced by a variety of early forms: '...de Grene', '...de la Grene'. '...del grene', '...attegrene' and '...on the grene' are recorded.

Turning to the whiteness of complexion or hair, less obvious references to these are **Hoare, Snow, Frost, Blunt** (from the French 'blond') and **Blanchard** (again from the French), while **Albin** may have been reserved for one with an especially pale complexion. **Blanchflower** ('white flower'), in its implication of a smooth, pale skin, like that of a young woman, may have been a most unwelcome sobriquet as the boy grew older, though of course it may just as easily have been applied to a girl. **Sherlock**, on the other hand, may have been a welcome and flattering label, for it meant 'shining locks'. **Fairfax** too, would not have been an unwelcome nickname, for it arose from two Old English words, 'fæger' and 'feax', which originally meant 'beautiful hair'.

In examining the other end of the colour scene, we might begin with some words of a general nature. **Dark(e)**, **Dunn(e)** and **Cole** all denoted a certain duskiness of appearance, indeed, **Cole** went further by likening the subject's complexion to charcoal, which is what 'col' originally meant. An unusually dark-skinned person might have been compared with a Moor (a native of Morocco), thus being described as 'moorish', which has become **Morris** and **Maurice**. **Morell** (of which there are several spellings) also has the same meaning – 'swarthy' we might say today.

Having mentioned nearly sixty colour-based surnames so far in this section, I have by no means exhausted the surnames we have acquired from colours and shades, which proves how resourceful and inventive our ancestors were in their descriptions and particularising of each other's heads and faces. Occasionally one comes across delightful examples of surnames still in use which retain their mediæval flavour and as a result, they stick in one's memory. Two such names with colour connotations are **Fairbeard** and **Dunbobbin** ('dark little Robert'). Neither of these names appears in the London telephone book, or my local directory, but there are 16 of the first and 125 of the second nationwide.

Beard is a common surname (there are 28 listed in the Oxford telephone directory), which may seem odd, since beards were not uncommon and would hardly have elicited comment unless there was some evident peculiarity of colour, shape, length or perhaps texture. Dr Reaney[1] has noted some delightfully descriptive nicknames, now alas, long forgotten: Thomas Dustibeard in 1229 (could this man have been a miller?), William Museberd in 1198 ('mouse beard', probably alluding to its colour), John Spadeberd in 1246 (spade-shaped beard) and Roger Thistliberd in 1260 (clearly a reference to its prickly texture). A curly texture to a man's beard would often give rise to the nickname **Crisp**, which has become curiously transformed in subsequent pronunciation into **Cripps**, as I have mentioned before.

We have now almost completed our tour of the head and face in search of surnames. One final look at the face leaves us with two accurate nicknames and a deceptive one. There are more examples of the surname **Tooth** to be found than one might expect, having been a nickname given to a child with prominent or misaligned front teeth (missing teeth were

---

1. P. H. Reaney (1979 edition) *The Origin of English Surnames*. Routledge & Keegan Paul.

probably too common to warrant mention). The London directory shows 7 entries for this name, with 83 further entries in the capital's electoral registers. Staffordshire, however, seems to be the hot-spot for this name. The nickname **Tong**, **Tonge** or **Tongue** was readily applied to a chatterbox but, as there are places of this name in several counties, the human organ is not the only source of the surname. The second deceptive name I mentioned at the beginning of this paragraph is **Gumm**, which is more often seen as **Gomme**. In spite of appearances, this name has nothing to do with the mouth, but comes from the Old English word 'guma' meaning simply 'a man'.

The Neck, Body and Legs

On moving from the face to the neck, we find very few surviving surnames. In Chapter One I mentioned a woman who was known as Edith Swan-neck (who was in fact, the mistress of King Harold who was killed at Hastings in October 1066). It is just possible that this name survives today in the surname **Swannick**, although as always, we must exercise caution, since there are two places called **Swanwick** (Derbyshire and Hampshire) and in both localities, the name has long been pronounced **Swannick**, so that the surname may have its origins in the place- names.

The rare surname **Whittles** (1 in the London telephone directory, though nearly 300 across the country) originates in the Old English words 'hwit hals', which meant 'white neck'. However, that final '-s' is of critical importance, for this surname must not be confused with the commoner name **Whittle**, which may have referred to one who dwelt on, or near, a 'white hill'. This meaning occurs in several place-names such as Welch Whittle and Whittle le Woods (both in Lancashire) as well as **Whittle** itself in Northumberland. **Neck** survives, notably in Surrey, Hampshire and Kent and we must assume that it was applied in cases of unusually long, thick, short or deformed necks. In the case of a short neck, this feature could be accommodated in the name **Neckles** (that is, 'neck-less'), a curious, but well-noted defect and still recorded in the London telephone book with 6 entries.

Great physical strength would naturally be a source of comment, as we will see from the frequency in our telephone books of the names **Strong**, **Strang** and **Armstrong**. Less much common, but perhaps more specifically descriptive, is the unusual name **Strongitharm**, with 4 entries in the London electoral records (and 2 in my local register). The name means 'strong-in-the-arm' of course, as does the name **Firebrace**, which may seem most unlikely, until we discover that the name is the Englishman's rendering of the French 'fier bras', meaning 'fierce-' or 'proud-arm'. There are several variations in the spelling of this surname, but national records show that **Fairbrass** has become the dominant version today, by a ratio of 4 to 1. One who was particularly broad across the back might have earned himself the straightforward nickname **Shoulder** or **Shoulders** – also a surname still in circulation. With over 150 entries in the London telephone directory, **Hand** and **Hands** must be considered common surnames. Again, a man who had especially strong or large hands, or one who had a peculiar deformity, would attract such a nickname. However, an alternative origin has been proposed, which suggests that the name may be a form of the German personal name Hans (a contraction of Johanns – John), which may account for **Hands**, but not for **Hand**. This reasoning appears rather feeble, I feel, and it seems to me more probable that **Hands** means what it says. The hands may also be recalled in the names **Maine**, **Maines**, **Mayne** and **Maynes** from the French for 'hand', as well as being a former province of Northwest France, from whence many mediæval immigrants must have arrived. An odd name in this group is **Quartermain** (French, 'quatre mains' – four-hands). This is probably another reference to physical strength, since it seems to allude to the mailed hands – the 'iron-hand'.

Back is not as unusual a surname as one might suppose, for there are over 200 bearers in the Greater London area. It too, has mixed origins. It may indeed have extolled one who possessed a strong physique, but it is more likely that the nickname was bestowed upon an unfortunate individual with a crooked spine or a hump. Another possible source of **Back** lies in the Old English personal name Bacca.

A part of the human anatomy (or perhaps I should say two parts) that generally escapes mention today is (are) the buttocks. I need hardly say that this feature was not spared the attention of our mediæval forebears. Apart from some horribly crude nicknames that found their way into records, possibly the only two names that have come down the ages to us and which relate to the buttocks are **Tout** and **Rump**. It is conceivable that their exact meanings had been forgotten by the ordinary folk and this may have helped them to survive the passage of the centuries, there being over 200 records of each across the kingdom. One cannot help wondering exactly what peculiarity could have provoked remark all those centuries ago.

Nicknames describing the belly were once frequent, but have, understandably, disappeared, with the exception of an unlikely one, **Pauncefoot**, which meant 'round belly'. I can find no current trace of it and it may have ceased to exist. Those having the surname **Bowell** will be relieved to find that their name has nothing whatever to do with our digestive organ, but has its roots in either the French town of Boulles, from where an early ancestor must have originated (**Bowles**, too may be a descendant of the same town), or else it has arisen from the Welsh 'ap

Howell' ('son of **Howell**') and is an alternative to **Powell**.

We are gradually travelling down the body and have now arrived at the legs and feet. The shape of a man's legs was more in evidence during the middle ages than today, the general custom of male attire being, amongst the peasantry at any rate, a simple over-garment reaching the knees, with hose or stockings beneath (if worn at all). Thus leg size and shape would be as likely to arouse comment as would the foot, hand or head. The usual reference to the legs was **Shanks**, which naturally attracted prefixes giving compounds like 'longshanks', 'shortshanks' and even 'sheepshanks' and 'dogshanks'. A rather amusing one was 'philipshanks', 'sparrow-legs'. A strong survivor of the '-shanks' group is **Crookshank** (**Cruikshank** as they have it in Scotland). Strangely enough, the Scottish form outnumbers the English form by almost 50 to 1 in the London telephone directory. Its meaning is clear: it would have been a nickname applied to one who had unusually crooked or bowed legs, through accident, disease or congenital deformity. **Legg** (also **Legge**) itself, is a fairly well-known surname and also drew attention to the shape or length of the bearer's legs, or perhaps to his fleetness of foot. One of the few '-legg' compounds to have survived the centuries is **Whitelegg**, which may have referred to the whiteness of a man's hose, or perhaps his white skin. It is a fairly rare surname nowadays with only 13 being recorded in the London electoral lists.

Bain and **Baines** are simply modified forms of **Bone** and **Bones** which usually referred to the legs and have produced the rather obvious compounds **Smallbone** ('small-legs') and **Longbone** (similar in meaning to 'longshanks'). **Knee** and **Kneebone** occur in small numbers still and probably drew attention to some deformity of the lower limbs.

And so we reach the foot, which has always given rise to remark and metaphor. **Foot** itself, could have implied almost anything from outstandingly large or small feet, deformed or crippled feet, to an exceptional nimbleness. In Chapter One, I referred to the 11th century Danish king of England, Harold Harefoot – an obvious reference to his remarkable agility. This and other such evocative nicknames as Dovefoot and Oxfoot have almost certainly become extinct. One which has not, however, is **Crowfoot**, as we see from the 4 examples listed in the London telephone directory. **Barefoot** (and **Barfoot**) are self-explanatory and **Lightfoot** tells of a sprightly ancestor, perhaps one who held the office of messenger to a court personage or a civic body. **Proudfoot** is an evocative name and must have been earned by one who walked with something of a swagger – most likely a well-to-do individual like Robert **Proudfoot**, Sheriff of London in about 1140[1]. **Pettifer,** from the French 'pied de fer', meant 'iron foot' and may have originated from one with a heavy-footed,

---

1. P. H. Reaney (1979 edition) *The Origin of English Surnames*. Routledge & Keegan Paul.

rolling gait, or perhaps from the wearing of an armoured shoe called a solleret.

Toe narrowly survives, with about 40 recorded bearers nationwide and may seem and unlikely organ for remark. The origin of the name, however, belongs in Chapter Four (Surnames From Local Features), for it referred to one who lived or worked on a high spur of land – a 'hoe' or 'how' – and is a contraction of 'at-ho'. Nevertheless, reference to speed and agility makes another appearance in the surname **Steptoe**, probably having its origin in the words 'step-to'. **Heale**, a relatively common name throughout Britain, has no connection with the foot, but is derived either from the Old English *healh*, meaning a secluded corner and would have been applied to a dweller in such a quiet nook, or to one originating from one of a number of small villages called Hele in the West Country.

We have now reached the end of our look at surnames arising directly from the body and its parts. However, I would like to append a small number of names that are deceptive in that they do not mean what they seem to say. **Heart**, for example, is nothing more than a variation of **Hart** (as is **Hurt**), a male deer and may be one of the many names implying a certain nimbleness, while the occasional **Lung** is really **Long**. **Brain**, we may feel is an unlikely surname. Its origin, however, has no connection with the cranial organ, which was little understood in mediæval days, but probably came from the name Bran, meaning 'raven' and was the name of a 9th century Celtic prince. Finally, the surname **Wombwell** springs, not from the female anatomy, but from the Yorkshire town of that name and meant 'a stream flowing through, or rising in a hollow'.

Deformities and failings of the human form

Having looked in some detail at the human physique and the great variety of shapes and sizes of its parts, as well as some of its imperfections, we can be sure that any deformities, weaknesses or losses of any part of it would soon have elicited appropriate nicknames from the neighbours. The incidence of children born with physical or mental defects must have been considerable (though dismally accepted), especially in the villages, after so many generations of limited movement and opportunity. However, most such specific nicknames were of a fleeting nature and faded from the memory some little time after the passing of their bearers. Nicknames applied to individuals with seriously defective bodies or minds would not, in most cases, be inherited, simply because the unfortunate soul would produce no offspring. In any case, the child of 'One-eye' would not wish to be burdened with a lifetime's reference to its parent's misfortune. Nevertheless, a faint memory of one or two of those defects is still lurking in a few of our surnames.

Perhaps the most commonly met name in the 'defects' group is **Crook.** Its frequency, however, is probably due as much to the several villages of this name as to those unfortunates whose backs were bent, humped or twisted. In some localities, a dweller at the bend (or crook) of a river might also have been known by this nickname. I mentioned a common compound of **Crook** in the form of **Crookshank** in the previous section (*The Neck, Body and Legs*). Other surnames that recall an ancient crookedness or malformation of limb or spine are **Cramp**, **Crump**, **Twist** and **Twiss**.

Lumps, swellings, bulges, boils, sores and numerous other disagreeable excrescences are common enough complaints today, even with the advantages of modern hygiene and medicine, but in mediæval times, with only herbs, charms, loathsome potions, prayers and, in the last resort, the crude amputating-saw, to offer any hope of effecting a cure, such repulsive sights must have been very familiar. Such disorders are remembered in the surname **Bunch**, which often also referred to a humped back, while the innocent-seeming **Bunney** was a word derived from the French and was commonly used for a swelling: 'a bony or grete knobbe' (1440)[1]. This should not be confused with **Bunny,** however, which combines the Old English elements 'bune' (a reed) and 'eg' (an island) to give 'a reed-island', clearly a location surname, as well as the name of a village in Norfolk.

Baldness may not be considered much of a handicap, but it has produced a few surnames which will have a familiar ring: **Ballard**, **Callow** and **Nott** come from Old or Middle English, while the names **Cave** and **Chaffe** are of French origin. Perhaps the commonest reminder in our surnames of ancestral baldness is **Ball**, while closely cropped hair is recalled in the name **Pollard**.

Finally, I will mention the surname **Twinn**. Though not a flaw of course, the appearance of twins was unusual enough to cause comment and was widely believed to be a sign of Almighty Displeasure or else an omen of ill luck. There are five entries of **Twinn** in my local telephone book.

Names flattering the human form

If our mediæval ancestors were forever ready to apply descriptive labels to those of their communities who bore physical imperfections, they were equally ready to give praise where it was due and were quick to recognise beauty and extol virtue. **Dainty** and its lisping variation **Dentith** come from a word meaning 'handsome or fine-featured', rather than 'delicate and fragile', as we would use dainty today. While **Bell** has an important

---

1. New English Dictionary – (Oxford 1888–1933).

origin in the French 'belle' ('beautiful', of face), its other sources show that it may have been an occupational nickname – a bell-maker or bell-ringer, or that it may have been acquired by one who lived or worked at the sign of the bell (that is at an inn or tavern), as in the recorded case of John atte Belle (1332)[1]. Continuing the 'belle' theme, two fairly common names are **Belcher** and **Bellamy**, each also having its root in the French word. **Belcher** is an Anglicisation of 'belle chiere' originally meaning 'fair of face', while **Bellamy** basks in the pleasure of 'belle ami' ('fair friend'). It is worth reminding ourselves that in mediæval times the word 'fair' meant 'pleasing' and even 'beautiful', where appropriate and in the following seven surnames we should bear this in mind. Most telephone books will yield a few entries of the surname **Fair** itself (the London 'phone directory gives 15), which probably implied a degree of handsomeness or beauty and which readily spawned a crop of compounds, among which are **Fairhead**, **Fairchild**, (**Fairbairn** is the Scottish form), **Fairbrother** and **Fairman,** none of which needs more explanation; nor does the unusual **Fairminer**, for this also means what it says. We might now ask whether there are any other occupations remembered in the same flattering terms. Probably the only one extant is **Fairgrieve,** which, though scarce, can be found in several telephone directories and meant 'handsome reeve' – the **Reeve** being the elected (or appointed) village foreman.

As an appendix to the above discussion, I'll mention two names which, though they begin with the syllable 'Fair-', do not belong to the above group at all, but they are interesting because they appear to be opposites and are not! They are **Fairfull** and **Fairless**. Surely their meanings are fairly obvious? Well, perhaps not quite. The first is really 'fair-fowl', that is, 'beautiful bird' and the second is a transformation of 'fearless', quite a flattering nickname, but rather on the abstract side (see a later section of this chapter for more of this type).

I think it must be evident to the reader by now that pre-Conquest English is the source of a considerable proportion of our surnames, amongst which are such nicknames as **Old**, **Young, Younger, Young-husband**, **Youngson**, **Youngman** and several others based on the 'Young-' prefix, all of which are refreshingly, self-explanatory. Two Latin adoptions, **Senior** and its converse **Junior** form an interesting comple-ment to the Old English pair of names at the beginning of the list in the first sentence of this paragraph. **Senior** must be considered the more common surname, since it rates 38 entries in the London telephone direc-tory, while **Junior** manages 12, making it a fairly rare name.

There are also many names beginning with 'Good-' in its familiar modern sense. Many speak for themselves and we may take as examples appropriate to this section **Goodbody, Goodhead,** and **Goodhand.**

And so, as we reach the end of our survey of surnames that are

---

1. P. H. Reaney (1976) *A Dictionary of British Surnames.* Routledge & Keegan Paul.

derived from mediæval nicknames relating to the human form, its virtues and its failings, we take our leave of one very personal source of names. I have not mentioned every surname belonging to this category of course, but those remaining will be fairly rare and often difficult to recognise at first sight for what they are, though they are no less interesting for that.

Temperament and character

One of Man's less endearing habits has always been to express his opinions freely about his fellows. Such gossiping about one another must have led to the formation of many a nickname, both complimentary and coarse. Indeed, we know from surviving records that many downright offensive names were used, though almost all have lasted no longer than their bearers, which may be a blessing. However, in spite of the distasteful nature of such epithets, they do allow us a glance into the thinking processes of our forebears, their invention and the range of colour attainable in their everyday language.

If we were living in the surname-forming period today, we would find that some of our modern expressions were beginning to stick to people whose features, physical or temperamental, were a little off the normal line. For example, a cantankerous and provoking manner is often nowadays called 'bolshie', a word which, despite its Russian language origin, has been enthusiastically embraced into English, while a haughty air is said to be 'snooty' (a reference here to the snout), or 'toffee-nosed'. A 'phoney' describes one who is pretentious and not what he seems, while a person who cannot be trusted to keep secrets might be called a 'blabber'. These words or developments of them, might easily find their way into future surnames and it is entertaining to speculate on the form they might take: perhaps Bolshey, Snutty, Toffin, Fony and Blabb are possibilities. A few minutes with a dictionary of slang could lead to a new and original line of predictive study from this point of view.

So, let's now examine the results of such tongue-wagging amongst the villagers and citizens of Mediæval England.

Flattering nicknames

To have been known by one's neighbours as 'god' – that is 'good' (leading to our surnames **Good** and **Goode**), must have generated a feeling of pleasure within the breast of the bearer. Of the many surviving surnames which are prefixed by 'Good-', I might mention **Goodfellow**, **Goodhew**, ('good Hugh'), **Goodlad** and **Goodhart** ('good heart'), as being pleasingly flattering and each of which crops up about a dozen times in the current London telephone book. More common than these, however, are **Goodchild** and **Goodman** – enviable nicknames! Mediæval England, being a male dominated society, seemed to have few nicknames specifically praising goodness in women. The electoral rolls now give no entries of **Goodmaid**, though it once existed. **Goodlass** may be a candidate for this group too, though it may also be a variation of 'god-less' – not such a flattering nickname.

The supremacy of Old English was soon to be challenged by the language brought by the recent conquerors from Normandy, so that by the end of the 12th century '… le Gode' and '… le Bon' were sharing common approval. Thus 'bon' began its penetration of the surname movement and from it has evolved a large number of surnames rivalling the native versions. The simplest is of course **Bone**, in which 'bon' has acquired a final 'e' (but see also the previous section, *The Neck, Body and Legs*). We might also include **Bonser** ('good sir') and **Bonham**, which looks as though it is a place-name, but is actually a well-disguised 'bon homme' – 'good man'. In addition to these, there are **Bonner** and **Bonar**, which people inclined to use in the sense of having a kind, gentle or courteous disposition, rather than simply 'good'. The chivalrous attributes of courtesy and grace are also recalled in the names **Curtis**, **Curtiss** and **Curtois**, but the name **Grace** itself, although it must sometimes have derived from a Middle English word 'gras', meaning 'charming', it is probably more often the result of the native pronunciation of the French 'grise', 'grey' and referred to hair colour.

A cheerful nature is recalled in a little crop of surnames: **Gay**, **Gaye**, **Merry**, **Sweet**, **Jolly**, **Jolley**, **Bligh**, **Blythe**, **Fairweather** and **Merryweather**, each having its own shade of meaning. **Sillman** and **Sellman** belong here too, for they meant 'happy man' (Old English 'sælig', that is, happy).

The pleasing and laudable trait of generosity is recognisable in the name **Large**, which is directly from the French and from which we also obtain the useful noun 'largesse'. Fine judgment find a memorial in the names **Wise**, **Wisdom**, **Sage** and the unexpected word **Ready** (and its variation **Reddy**). The Saxon king of England Ethelred II, whose unhappy reign at the turn of the 10th century resulted in the massacre of a large number of Danish settlers in eastern England in 1002, was well nicknamed 'The Unready', that is, lacking wisdom. In our modern usage, 'ready' has lost its original specific meaning of shrewd judgment, in favour of a more general preparedness or willingness.

Bravery, an attribute universally esteemed, if not always generally sought, has been the source of many names, among the most familiar of which are **Bold, Courage, Doughty, Hardiman, Harding, Hardy** (these last three meaning 'courageous man'), **Manly**, **Stout** and **Prowse** (from the Old French 'prous' – valiant). Another name which must, I think, take its place here, is **Turnbull**. Any man who could really have turned a bull single-handedly, which is what the name seems to have meant, would have deserved hearty acknowledgment from his fellows and such a feat must have been a lively talking point for many a day, remaining in folk's memories and eventually passing into local folklore. I have heard the name **Turnbull** pronounced as both **Trumble** and **Tumble** in different parts of England, while retaining the initial spelling.

Another knightly attribute was loyalty – a virtuous complement to bravery – and this too, has given rise to small group of surnames: **Truman** ('loyal man'), **Tromans**, **Faith** and **Faithfull**. Similarly, a single-minded and steadfast character was also worthy of recognition and the names **Steele**, **Stern** and **Stark** applaud this quality.

Some surnames shout their meanings loud and clear. **Dear**, **Dearlove** and **Darling** are unmistakable in their expression of devoted affection, all having their roots in the Old English 'dœre'. To these we may add the less obviously related **Mullings** and **Leafe**. The word 'mulling' was the Old English for 'darling', but has become hopelessly confused with **Mullins**, which recalled one who lived or worked 'at the mill'. **Leafe** (or **Leaf**) also come from an Old English word 'leof', meaning 'beloved', while Old French provides us with the name **Paramore** ('par amour') and was used for 'sweetheart'. A complimentary nickname (for a woman!) deriving from the word 'husewyf' (a housewife, indicating a good manager and mistress), gives us the surname **Hussey** and is quite different in origin from the derogatory word 'hussy', a minx or Jezebel.

Some noteworthy act must have occasioned the nickname **Makepeace**, a surname that is rather more common in the north of England than elsewhere. Indeed, both Northumberland and Durham are the present-day strongholds of the name.

What better way to end this section on flattering nicknames than with the ultimate in complimentary titles, the highest merit achievable, the most flattering sentiment that can surely find expression about any individual? **Parfitt** is that name. It is not of home-grown origin, however, for it is from the French 'parfait', that is, 'perfect'. Unfortunately (I feel) it has eclipsed **Faultless**, of which few remain, even in its modern-day haven around Birmingham and the West Midlands, though there is a lone entry in my local telephone book. We may well wonder about the sort of person to whom his or her fellows applied this best of all nicknames and the qualities which so impressed them. Small wonder that the surname was not discarded by the generations that followed.

Disparaging nicknames

Some nicknames that were originally unflattering and probably unwelcome to those on whom they were conferred have, by luck, survived, though the majority of such names must have been gladly abandoned long ago as inherited surnames and understandably so. One can imagine the sons of William le Cruel (1251), Ralph Snivel (1206) and Thomas le Spewer (1247)[1] readily shedding such references in favour of something less disagreeable. Those names that *have* come down to us may well have survived because their original meanings were forgotten.

Those individuals of a proud and haughty nature might well have earned themselves the nicknames **Proud** (and **Prout**) and less evidently, **Hawtin**. 'Know-alls' or 'big-heads', as we would call them today, were sometimes rewarded with the nickname **Tester**, from the Old French 'testard', while a cunning, slippery scamp's burden would perhaps have been **Pratt**. If his cunning was of a distinctly monetary or commercial nature, the word 'barat' was favoured and it is from this that we have the surnames **Barrat** and **Barrett** (and several variations). This individual seems to have been the mediæval equivalent of the mid-20th century 'spiv', 'wide-boy' or 'chancer', though often **Fox** or **Todd** would have been enough to describe such a character.

The mention of **Barrat** will remind us that there is a group of surnames that recall those who had dealings with money in some way, either in the course of their occupations or as borrowers, lenders or hoarders. One who was notoriously 'tight-fisted' or who pursued wealth, most probably would have been simply **Money**, while **Moneypenny** (really 'many-penny'), although not all that common a name today, harks back to the profiteer, as does **Turnpenny**, but **Pennyfeather** ('penny-father') perpetuates the memory of one who hoarded his coins – a miser, in short. As I have mentioned already, an element of irony is often present in the Englishman's humour and the four nicknames above might easily have been given to those who always seemed to be without money of their own, though **Poor(e)** was a common and straightforward name for this impecunious condition. A lender, or worker at one of the many official mints has given us the rather rare name **Monier.**

Laziness would naturally bring forth a number of sharp sobriquets, some of which I can't help smiling over: Geoffrey Liggbiyefyre ('lie-by-the-fire'), Thomas Sitequyt ('sit-quiet'), Geoffrey Sitadun ('sit-down') and Henry Leaealday ('lean-all-day')[2] all lived during the surname-forming period and it is amusing to think that perhaps their descendants live today unaware of the indolent dispositions of their mediæval forefathers. There must be many such unexpected skeletons locked away forever in our ancestral cupboards! However, we have inherited at least

---

1. P. H. Reaney (1979 edition) *The Origin of English Surnames*. Routledge & Keegan Paul.

2. P. H. Reaney (1979 edition). *The Origin of English Surnames*. Routledge & Keegan Paul.

four names which reflect a certain easy-going lethargy: **Dolittle**, which is embarrassingly self-explanatory, **Langrish** (one meaning is 'lazy', another originates in the place-name Langrish in Hampshire), **Goodenough** (a surprisingly common name in my district with 22 entries in the telephone book), which describes one easily satisfied, while **Toogood**, with its touch of sarcasm, probably meant the same as **Goodenough**.

Two words whose exact meanings were possibly forgotten early on, have given us the surnames **Dwelly** and **Gulliver**. The first has its root in the Old English adjective 'dweollic', which meant 'foolish and weak-minded', while the second, **Gulliver**, is of French ancestry and meant 'a glutton'. Of the two, **Gulliver** is by far the most common and is familiar to us from Jonathan Swift's 1726 satire, 'Gulliver's Travels'.

An habitually clumsy or awkward person might well have been referred to as **Gawke** and indeed, we still use the word 'gawky' to describe a young, ungainly blunderer, the growth of whose limbs seems to have run ahead of the rest of his or her body. The origins of the name are uncertain. Perhaps its source lies in the French 'gauche', which means 'awkward, clumsy'. The surname is certainly now very rare; there is only one listed in the Northwest Kent telephone book and none at all in the London directories, though there are 16 electoral register entries of the name for England.

Three grim nicknames

Three surnames hiding under a cloak of innocence, but which may conceal an ancient grim reality, are **Brent** (sometimes seen as **Brend**), **Brennan(d)** and **Spendlove**. The name **Brent** itself, could mean 'burnt' (though there are several villages whose names incorporate the word **Brent**) and **Brennan(d)** is a contraction of the words 'burnt-hand'. These two names may be macabre reminders of one of the punishments administered for theft – that is, branding. **Spendlove** looks harmless enough but, although it could sometimes refer to one who was notably free with his (or her) affections, it also has a more sinister origin: coming from an Old French expression, 'espand louve', to disembowel.

Abstract nicknames

There is a small collection of names which are mostly of a completely abstract nature and which are largely complimentary or at least, inoffensive. **Bliss**, **Blessed**, **Comfort** and **Plenty** all retain their original meanings, while **Love** might have referred either to the emotion or to a she-wolf (French, 'louve')! **Raison** and **Reason** must often have meant 'reason', but could also have described bodily strength because the Old English word 'ræson' meant 'a beam' – presumably implying stoutness and vigour. **Theedom** and **Theedam**, from a Middle English noun which meant 'prosperity', represent perhaps a case of parental wishful thinking.

One of the few surviving names from this group with a distinctly unflattering flavour is **Atter** (and **Attar**) which, despite its benign appearance, is derived from 'etor', which meant 'poison, bitterness' and even 'venom' and we may wonder about the reasons for the conferring of such a nickname. Could it have been applied to one with a spitefully sharp tongue? It is a fairly rare name now (though one which I have personally encountered in the east London area), rating 13 entries in the current London telephone directory.

As a youngster, I remember being puzzled by the word embossed on a two-gallon petrol tin – **Carless**. I thought it probably stood as a warning that a motorist would be car-less if he ran out of the fluid it contained. The name, of course, means 'careless' in its literal sense of 'care-free' and 'light-hearted'. There are several other abstract words having the suffix '-less' and which have survived the passage of the centuries. **Lawless** is one and could suggest a wild and unbridled spirit, as well as an outlaw or other law-breaker. **Loveless** and its variant **Lovelace**, undoubtedly meant what they said in some instances, but in others they would have been applied in irony to one who was an habitual flirt or had had many loves.

The vices, such as lust, envy and sloth may once have given rise to nicknames which, perhaps understandably, were soon abandoned, though the London telephone directory lists **Pride** (and **Pryde**) (13), **Greed** (1) and **Greedy** (1). These surnames must often have had their origins in the mediæval pageants where actors were often associated with the roles they played every year. **Jellow** and **Jallow** probably reflect the distasteful vice of jealousy and come from the Middle English word 'jalous'.

After all those unsettling names, let me end this segment on a lighter and more cheerful note with four names expressive of healthy optimism. **Faith** and **Peace** have both made a modest impression on our surnames, each appearing about 10 times in the London telephone books. The all-embracing **Virtue** (**Vertue** too) is less common (2). The surname which wins the performance honours by a grand margin, however, is **Hope** (210 listed in the London telephone directory), which is perhaps as it should be and allows us to end our look at abstract surnames on an optimistic note.

Nicknames from dress

In Chapter Two, when mentioning Robin Hood, I remarked that **Hood** and **Hod** had the same meaning – 'hod' being the more usual mediæval word for a hood. These words must often have been used as nicknames for wearers of hoods that were somehow distinctive: colour, length or shape for instance, as well as being applied to the maker of the garment. **Capp**, **Cape** and **Cope** are also as likely to have been the names given to the wearer of a distinctive head covering as to the cap-maker himself. However, there can be little doubt that the names **Hoodless** and **Hodlass** (each meaning 'hood-less'), like **Shorthouse** (that is, 'short-hose', stockings), were simple, direct nicknames describing a peculiarity of habit.

Costume and dress have left us with relatively few names, though there were originally more, as we might expect. As far as the peasantry was concerned, dress had a more or less general plainness and was hardly worthy of comment. It was the better-off whose attire was much more likely to catch the attention, producing such names as William Redschoz ('red-shoes', 1332) and John Furhode ('fur-hood', 1301)[1]. So, why is it that the names **Shorthouse** and **Hoodless** have survived (in small numbers, it is true), when other, equally descriptive names like Blacsleve ('black-sleeve'), Letherhose ('leather-breeches'), Witkertel ('white-gown') and Heighschoo ('high-shoe') have long since vanished? The explanations lie in the simple facts that:

(i)   families bearing these names died out;
(ii)   there had been no male heirs to the names;
(iii)   the original names had been changed;
(iv)   the nicknames may have been applied to women;
(v)   the nicknames were transient and too early in the surname-forming period to persist.

It is certainly a fact that our surname register would have been the richer and more colourful had we inherited even one-tenth of those names lost after the year 1300.

Nicknames from animals

"A wise old owl lived in an oak ....", goes the rhyme; "With cat-like tread ....", sing the policemen in 'The Pirates of Penzance'; "As stubborn as a donkey", goes the saying; ".... at a snail's pace, moving crab-wise and

---

1. P. H. Reaney (1979 edition) *The Origin of English Surnames*. Routledge & Keegan Paul.

looking sheepish" and so on.

There are hundreds of references to animals and their natures in our language. In our imaginations we can all see the stealth of a stalking cat and anyone whose movements were observed to be feline would soon find himself likened to a cat, hence the rare surnames **Catt**, **Catte** and **Chatt**. Add a touch of cunning and the nickname becomes **Fox** instead. A naturally 'foxy' look or even a head of fox-coloured hair might also draw forth the same nickname. In some northern districts **Todd** was the usual name for the fox.

With 119 entries in the London telephone directory, **Wolf(e)** and **Wolff** must be considered a pretty common surname. It occurs in disguised form in a number of words, and features strongly in a large number of pre-Conquest personal names, as well as some names from the Continent. The wolf was a creature held in great mystical respect by Saxon inhabitants of England and for a man to be compared to a wolf was highly gratifying and complimentary. Here are some 'wolf' surnames together with their original personal names, where applicable and their meanings:

Wolfitt	– Wulfgeat, 'wolf-great';
Wolfson	– 'Son of Wulf';
Woolgar	– Wulfgar, 'wolf-spear';
Woollard	– Wolfweard, 'wolf-guardian';
Woolley	– Wolf-leah, 'wolf-wood';
Woolmer	– Wolfmær, 'wolf-famous';
Woolner	– Wulfnoth, 'wolf-bold';
Woolrich, **Wooldridge**, **Ulrich**	– Wulfrich, 'wolf-powerful';
Woolsey	– Wulfsige, 'wolf-victory'.

I will have more to say about such names as these in Chapter Eight. Some of the original literal meanings of the names like **Woolgar** and **Woolmer** may seem curious to us. What on earth is a 'wolf-spear' and what can 'wolf-famous' possibly mean? The answers are to be found in the 10th century custom of combining one element of the father's name – in this case, Wulf – with one of that of the mother. The result is usually literal nonsense, but it was in the solemn belief and hope that these names would infuse the boy-child with a spirit of fearless vigour and courage, mingled with an element of restless defiance in the face of life's challenges, that these names were given and were thus highly acceptable.

The surnames listed above are only a few of the many names of this type that are current. One last 'wolfish' name I would like to add, though its origins lie in the so-called Anglo-French word 'louve' (a female wolf), is **Lovell**, literally 'little wolf, wolf-cub'.

Two other names inspiring to the imaginations of the early mediæval Englishman were **Boar** and **Hogg**, creatures that exhibited an enviable stubborn fearlessness in tight corners. Their aggressive temperament strongly appealed to our ancestors and the words became absorbed into the nomenclature. **Boar** is now rare – indeed there are no entries in the London telephone directory (though 2 are in the London electoral record), but **Hogg** occurs nearly 100 times.

A youth who grew into a man of great strength, perhaps coupled with a somewhat unpredictable temper, may have earned for himself the nickname **Bull**, a name he may have been pleased to bear. A similar idea is seen in the name **Bullock** and surprisingly, **Stott**, which was used for both bullock and stallion. A less welcome nickname to the youth of the time was **Lamb**, with its implication of meekness, an unwelcome notion in an age of bold and legendary folk-heroes and battle stories of valorous knights. The same can probably be said of **Meek** and **Meekly**. Although such nicknames could easily be given to girls of course, they are much less likely to have been inherited from the female partner of a marriage.

Lion and **Lyon** may have originated from stories (or even rare experiences) of the fierce nature of the wild animal itself, from its appearance in armorial insignia or from the picture on an inn sign. If the name is **Lyons**, however, it almost certainly owes its origin to an expatriate of the French town of Lyons-le-Forêt. **Leppard** would have been a fitting nickname for one who was agile, supple and swift of foot like the leopard, though few Englishmen can ever have seen one in the flesh. Otherwise its source may lie, like that of **Lion**, either in an heraldic device or was conferred on one who lived or worked at an inn on whose sign was a painted representation of the animal.

In another locality, a lively young stripling would have been called a **Kidd**, while **Buck** and **Roe** (**Rae** and **Ray** are the likely Scottish forms) also told of the youthful nimbleness familiar to our mediæval forebears of these woodland creatures.

Brock has a number of origins, only one of which alludes to the badger. It seems probable that in the animal context, **Brock** may not have been a welcome nickname, for 'the stinking brock' was a phrase familiar to mediæval folk, so the name may have been readily applied to one whose body stench was particularly rank. (Personal hygiene amongst even the nobility was, to our minds, very lax indeed, bathing being an activity rarely performed, so that sour and fœtid body smells were normal amongst both peasants and townsfolk). However, an alternative origin of **Brock** is that it became a variation of **Brook**, in which case we have a local feature name, near to which a villein had his dwelling. The name **Badger** itself, was often used as a nickname for a general hawker of goods like cloth and corn.

Coney (a rabbit), probably referred to a catcher of these animals for their skins, or to the artisan who worked their fur into garments, for it is difficult to think of any feature of a man's behaviour or appearance that could resemble that of a rabbit.

Foale and **Pullen** (French, 'poulain', a colt) would seem to belong to the same category that includes **Kidd, Buck, Roe** and **Leppard**, in that it suggests a friskiness characteristic of so many young animals. Even **Purcell** could imply this, for it meant 'a piglet' (French, 'porc', plus the diminutive suffix '-ell').

Between them, cats, dogs and horses have left us with surprisingly few surnames, which is not easy to explain, since these, together with chickens, were perhaps the most familiar of all the animals to be found in both village and town.

Most names beginning with 'Cat-' will have three possible origins:

(i) Pet forms of Catherine, like **Catt, Cattle, Cattell, Catlin** and **Catanach**;

(ii) Names derived from an ancient personal name such as **Caton** ('Cada's settlement'), **Catesby** ('Kati's village') and **Catsley** (Catoc's dwellings in the clearing or wood);

(iii) Place-names that alluded to wild cats such as **Catford, Catfield, Cattishall** and **Catton**.

Three interesting cat-names are **Puscat** (of which I find no trace now in any current mainland telephone directory, which may indicate its recent extinction), **Pussmaid**, a delightful name which is approaching the same fate as **Puscat**, since it is some years now that the telephone book for Severnside listed the only English example. Its original application may have been to a wilful and impish young girl – a 'minx' perhaps. The third cat-name is **Pussett**, also probably on the verge of vanishing for ever, for again, it is some time since the only example I could find appeared in the electoral lists for Tamworth, near Birmingham. This name has the typical French diminutive suffix '-ett' and as a nickname, it implied 'little puss'.

The only Two names one is likely to come across connected with the dog are **Doggett**, 'dog-head' – not a very flattering nickname, though a descriptive one all the same and **Terrier**, of which I can find 13 in electoral lists.

Surnames beginning with 'Hors-' nearly all refer to the animal, either directly or by way of a place-name: **Horseman** (and **Horsman**), **Horsley** ('horse-pasture', Derbyshire), **Horsey** ('horse-island', Norfolk) and **Horsnell** ('horse-nail', a maker of horseshoe nails, or a shoer of horses). An exception to this pattern is **Horsington** (Lincolnshire, but not the Somerset one, which has been shown to have been the 'settlement of Horsa's people'[1]).

Nicknames from insects

There can be small wonder that insects have played only a trivial role in the formation of our surnames. There is only a small handful of names which have sprung from mediæval names for insects. According to the London electoral registers, by far the most common name we have inherited in this context is **Budd** (well over 200 were listed on my last count), which came to be the word for a beetle (Old English 'budda'). The word's original meaning, however, was 'fat or plump' and it is in this respect that it accounts for so many instances in the records. Next in frequency comes **Breese** (also seen as **Breeze**), which derives from 'brœsa', a gadfly – a most distressing plague to cattle, but this does seem to be an important, though curious, source of the name. Another possible origin of **Breese** lies in the Welsh language. As I described in Chapter Five (Names of relationship), until the Welsh began to adopt the English system of surnaming in the early part of the 16th century, their formula for showing father to son relationship was to use 'ap' followed by the father's personal name. Thus 'ap **Rhys**' (son of Rhys) would soon condense into **Preece** and even **Breese**. So we must take this late development in the history of our surnames into consideration in this instance.

An original English word for a beetle was 'wicga', which has evolved into the name **Wigg** and which we can still find in our word 'earwig', while 'lobbe' was the spider and has given us **Lobb**. Quite how such nicknames were originally earned is a matter for our fancy – just what it is that makes schoolboys call each other Maggot, Grub and Bluebottle (all to my own knowledge) is hard to say when their own names bear no resemblance to the acquired nickname. It is clearly an ancient practice. The nickname **Bee**, however, must have been bestowed upon a busy, industrious fellow.

Bugg(e) is a surname which is not as uncommon as we might think, for there is a total of 99 in the London electoral lists and it looks as though it too, ought to belong here amongst the insect-surnames. However, it may be a relief those bearing the name that its origins are not at all creepie-crawlie. It has two alternative origins: the first arises from the word 'burgh', a borough, which may have meant no more than its original bearer was simply a citizen, a freeman or a man of local standing. The second source is in an occupational name deriving from the Old English word for 'scarecrow', a village lad given the task of scaring off birds from

---

1. E. Ekwall (1960 edition) *Concise Oxford Dictionary of Place Names.* Clarendon Press.

young growing crops.

So, only five surnames in this section have their origins in the insect-sized world – not surprising really.

Nicknames from birds

Unlike the insects, whose influence on our surnames has been minimal, the birds have taken our names by storm and have provided us with nearly sixty surnames. There are three reasons for the appearance of birds' names in nicknames:

(i)   a person's looks or behaviour might resemble those of a particular bird;

(ii)   a person might live or work at a tavern on whose sign was painted a bird;

(iii)   it may have been a man's occupation to catch, sell or train certain birds.

As we shall see from the table of frequencies at the end of this section, our once most common bird, the **Sparrow**, is by no means the commonest bird-nickname and comes a long way down the list. It was a name that might well have been earned by a lively character who had perhaps, a rather pointed nose. The **Starling** tends to be rather quarrelsome and noisy, and the **Jay** is gaudy and showy. The **Peacock**, also a showman, struts around pompously, fully aware of his station in life. The names **Pocock** and **Poe** are variations on the word **Peacock**. A love-lorn youth might have gained the nickname **Dove** or it may have been given to one who was gentle in manner (if he was not already afflicted with the nickname **Lamb**!) The other extreme of temperament was represented by the name **Hawk(e)**, who may have had a savage streak, or who simply had hawk-like features. The surname **Sparrowhawk** is not as uncommon a name as one may have thought; even my local telephone book lists 16 of them. Its numbers may be augmented if one takes into account the occasional local contraction of the word into **Spark(e)**, though the Old Norse word 'sparkr', meaning 'cheerful, sprightly', may be a significant contributor to this latter surname.

A formidable bird of prey was the **Eagle** and there is some evidence that the surname arose by the likening of an individual's aggressive temperament to that of this bird. Again, an inn sign incorporating a painting of an eagle probably gave rise to the nickname in some places, though another possibility is that an émigré of the French town of Laigle was called after the place of his origin, which easily transforms into **Eagle** in speech.

In some districts a young male hawk was known as a 'tercel' and it is from this word that the name **Tassell** has evolved, probably as an encouraging nickname. **Muskett** is the French-derived equivalent of **Tassell**.

Birds whose names have given us particularly complimentary surnames are varied. **Nightingale** was probably applied to a boy, though not necessarily so, with a sweet singing voice. Similarly, **Thrush** sang melodiously and may well have been a young man. In some districts he would have been nicknamed **Thrussell** (or **Throssell**) instead. As a youngster, I remember the bird itself referred to as the 'whistle-throstle' in my home district in Worcestershire. **Finch** must have been a cheery, alert little chap who went about his tasks whistling to himself, while **Wren** was small and good-natured, if a little nervous and retiring. The blue tit was once known as the titmouse and this word has turned itself into **Titmus**, an agile, chirpy little fellow.

Of course, such names as these were often given to children by loving parents in a mood of playful affection, a custom which continues today to some extent. I still hear the occasional 'chick' used in a friendly way by the older folk in my home district: "Hello chick, how are you?" However, this seems unknown in the south of the country where 'duck' is preferred: "Hello my duck". Londoners, especially Cockneys, are rather more likely to say "…. ducks", or "….cock", or even "… me ol' cock sparrer".

Less complimentary sentiments must have been intended by those who conferred on a neighbour the nicknames **Crow** and **Rook**, though **Rook** was also a corruption of 'oak' and may have indicated a dweller beside a notable oak tree. The birds' black cloaks and loud, unrefined and grating voices could easily have led a peasant to use them as descriptive nicknames on occasion. The magpie survives in the surname **Pye**, alluding to a cheeky opportunist who, in those far-off times, may even have been a little light-fingered too. **Pye** has several other possible origins which were discussed in the section on 'Food' in Chapter Two. The **Raven** too, like its three cousins above has a raucous voice and a black coat, but with a distinctive steely sheen, to which the smooth black hair of a person may have been compared. Mediæval boys must also have found that ravens could be quite easily tamed, making intelligent, but thievish pets.

The **Woodcock** was often regarded by mediæval folk as a foolish bird rather like the **Coot(e)**, the application of which nickname may also have implied a certain baldness. **Crane** and **Heron** were, in all probability, earned by men having long, spindly legs or even a long neck. The quail, which has evolved into the fancier name-form **Quayle**, stirred a variety of feelings in different places: sometimes it was considered something of a silly character, sometimes a shy fellow and in other places it was credited with an amorous nature. The surname **Swann** comes down to us either from the bird itself – its long white neck must often have inspired its application as a nickname (Edith Swan-neck is mentioned in both Chapter One and Chapter Seven) – or from the Old English word for a peasant or villager, 'swān', from which word we have also obtained the surname **Swain.**

Other bird names appearing in our surnames are **Cock** and **Cox, Cockerill**, a strutting, self-important fellow and of course, **Bird** itself, the most frequently occurring member of this group, which must have been the nickname of one whose features resembled those of a bird (small bright eyes, pointed nose, quick movements ….). **Drake** may have come from the male duck or from the 'draca', the dragon on the battle standard implying a standard bearer. **Duck**, **Swallow** and **Partridge** are clearly from the birds' names and may have signified the catchers of these birds.

From the French word for a parrot ('papegai') we have the unusual surname **Pobjoy**. The surname **Parrott**, paradoxically, comes, not from the bird, but from the French name Pierrot, meaning 'little Peter'. The rare name **Blackbird** is also deceptive, for it comes from 'black-beard'. In the London electoral records there are 8 bearers of the delightful surname **Pyefinch**, a colloquial name for the chaffinch and a clear case of mediæval parental affection it would seem.

To sum up the frequencies of birds' names in the London telephone directory (the numbers will change slightly with every publication of course), here is a table which could be compared with any other locality in order to detect regional variations or bias:

Bird, **Birds**, **Burd** 538
Finch 344
Peacock, **Pocock**, **Poe** 309
Cock(s), **Cox**, **Cockerill** etc 238
Drake 220
Crane 202
Crow(e) 177
Partridge 168
Swan(n) 165
Jay(e) 141
Woodcock 140
Dove 134
Hawk(e), **Hawkes**, **Hawker** 132
Nightingale 129
Wren(n) 118
Sparrow 115
Rook(s), **Rooke(s)** 114
Coot(e) 104
Raven 90
Eagle(s) 87

Pye (that is, the magpie) 84
Heron 67
Starling 64

Swallow, **Duck**, **Quail** (and **Quayle**), **Thrussell**, **Titmus**, **Lark(e)**, **Sparrowhawk**, **Pobjoy** and **Pyefinch** all appear fewer than 50 times each. I was interested to note that the name **Sparrowhawk** occurs 16 times in my local directory but only 8 times in the London book, showing a definite regional vigour. Of course, the ultimate check on the frequency of names in general is to carry out a survey using all of the British electoral rolls. In these days of sophisticated computer analysis and with so many records being available over the internet, the task is very much easier than it once was.

Our London survey shows just how many familiar birds' names still appear in our surnames and serves also to remind us of the part wild birds played in the lives of the mediæval English. Of course, many wild birds were caught for food and formed a familiar item in the diets of villagers and citizens alike; we read of blackbirds, thrushes, larks, pigeons, ducks, partridges, quail and pheasants, among others, being sold at town markets across the kingdom.

Finally, the earlier mention of the pleasing name **Pyefinch** brings me to a group of names which, at first sight, do not look like birds' names at all. The words in this group represent some of the more regional mediæval names given to familiar birds.

Regrettably, these words have fallen out of everyday usage, though they do crop up as the occasional interesting surname and are worth looking at, if only to see what we have lost:

Coe	– a jackdaw;
Culver	– a dove or pigeon;
Dunnock	– a hedge sparrow (a very shy little bird);
Pinnock	– a hedge sparrow again, also a blue tit (an agile little chap);
Povey	– a barn owl;
Puttock & Puttick	– a kite or buzzard (fierce and ruthless);
Ruddock, Ruddick & Reddick	– a robin redbreast;
Speight	– a woodpecker (it may have been a waggish name for a carpenter, as was **Peck** in some cases, though this word often referred to a sharp nose);
Spink	– a finch (after its pinking note). **Spink** was also a name for the wild flower now generally called 'lady's smock'.

A few other bird names can be found occasionally, but here I think we must say our goodbyes to Jenny Wren, Robin Redbreast, Mag Pye, Jack Daw, Tom Tit and of course, Dickie Bird.

Nicknames from fish

In the opinion of at least two distinguished experts in the study of surnames (C. L. Ewen and Canon C. W. Bardsley), no surname has been taken directly from a fish. They maintain that fish-surnames arise either as variations of other names, such as place-names or from occupations. This may well be the case since there can be few features an individual ever had in common with a fish and therefore there could rarely have been any reason to liken a person to one. However, the above-mentioned authorities' opinions are not quite set in stone and there may be some debatable exceptions to their thinking, as we shall see.

Many fish-surnames can be found in the telephone books and it might be interesting to examine the names and try to determine their origins.

The surname **Pike** (its variation is **Pyke**) has at least three sources: the most obvious one must be from the seller of fish, though not exclusively pike of course. I can't help feeling that a very thin and cadaverously narrow face might have been compared to that of this relatively familiar river fish, but this conflicts with the learned thinking of most authorities. A second origin of the name may lie in the Old English word 'pīc', which meant 'a point' and could have referred to one who lived on a hilltop. Thirdly, a tall, thin individual might have been likened by his fellows to a soldier's pikestaff. **Chubb** likewise, has a mixture of possible origins, even more diverse than those of **Pike.** In the first place, the word was sometimes used to describe a plump and slow-witted person and one could believe it was because the chub is indeed a fat little river fish – we still describe a plump person as 'chubby'. Here, however, we are again up against the views of the distinguished authorities, but with something of a case, perhaps. After that almost too obvious an explanation, we come to a second origin in which the name may have arisen from a colloquial form of the Biblical personal name **Job**, a man, we are told, of great patience and tolerance. A close phonetic relative of **Chubb** is **Jubb** and the source of this is in a French word meaning 'a foolish fellow', so that the two names may be variations of each other. Lastly, **Chubb** could well have connections with the maker of four-gallon vessels called 'jobbes'.

More straightforward than the last two names in their origins are **Bream** and **Brill**. The first has its root in an Old English word 'breme', which meant 'famous or fierce', while the second surname is a place-name – a hilltop village in Buckinghamshire. **Mullett**, though the name of a fish, is almost certainly derived from the street cries of mediæval Normandy mussel-sellers – 'Moulettes!' and selling their wares in post-Conquest southern English towns. **Herring**, too may have sold his fish by shouting the word across the town, thus earning himself a fishy nickname.

The **Roach** is a well-known game fish, but the surname may simply have arisen from a re-spelling of the French **Roche**, 'a rock', thus recording the location, a prominent rock, near to which was the dwelling of a particular person. **Haddock** probably *was* a catcher or seller of this fish, unless he had been a native of the Lancashire village of **Haydock**.

There are several spellings of the surname **Salmon**, including **Salomon** and **Sammond(s)**. They are nothing to do with the fish of that name, but are all variations of the Biblical name **Solomon**. **Spratt** too, is unconnected with the little bristling which we usually call the sprat, but is an alternative spelling of the name **Sprott**, a young shoot or bud (that is, a sprout) and was clearly a pet name. Also having no kinship with the fish of the same names are **Tunney** and **Hake**. These both owe their existence to two Old English personal names, Tunni and Haco.

The majority of the fish surnames I have mentioned so far are, as Ewen and Bardsley assert, clearly derived from occupations or other sources. The occupational element is probably also true of **Tench** and **Sturgeon**, two fairly rare surnames these days (there is one of each listed in my local 'phone book and only a few more in the London telephone directory). The flat, sleek **Tench** and the shark-like **Sturgeon** would seem to have little to offer in the way of human comparison, so that the most reasonable conclusion is that the nicknames arose from catchers or keepers of these fish. The double value of latter fish was in its flesh and its eggs (caviar) of course, and when the females returned to freshwater to spawn, they were caught and released into lakes, protected by weirs, under the guardianship of appointed keepers. King Edward II, a great lover of sturgeon flesh, issued a decree in 1324 declaring it to be a royal fish and therefore under the monarch's protection.

We may wonder at the character of a man nicknamed **Sharkey** by his fellows, but those bearing this surname need have no qualms: there is no connection with the fish! The surname derives from the mediæval Englishman's pronunciation of the Irish O'Searcaigh, that is, 'descendant of Searcach', which meant 'loving' in Irish Gaelic.

Although not fish of course, **Whale** and **Dolphin** can take their places in this section. There are 182 **Whale(s)** and 86 **Dolphin(s)** to be found in the electoral lists for London, showing that these surnames are comfortable survivors. One who had a slow, rolling gait, coupled perhaps with a distinct stoutness of physique may have been dubbed **Whale**, while **Dolphin** and its smoother version **Duffin,** had nothing to do with the aquatic mammal, but derived from the once popular 11th century Norse personal name Dolgfinnr.

I've left the most obvious name until last – **Fish** itself. Its frequent occurrence points to a nickname often applied, like **Fisher**, to the catcher and seller of fish, familiar occupations. Alternatively, it may have been jokingly applied to one with a persistent taste for fish.

On the whole, it looks as though our two learned authors mentioned at the start of this section are right: almost all fish names derive from occupations or have some other origin. However, there may just be a case to be made for a couple of nicknames directly applicable from the fish, though no one can be certain, of course.

Nicknames from flowers

In Chapter Four, we saw that certain trees, some of which were conspicuous local landmarks, readily found their way into surnames at an early stage: the ash, oak, birch, beech, holly and hazel became familiar elements in peoples' names and even the yew, hawthorn and willow have made a modest contribution. We might reasonably wonder therefore, whether other plants' names have been adopted into surnames through the early nicknaming process. This has not been the case, however, for almost all plant-names that *do* appear in our surnames (and there are not many of them) have their original influence outside the plant kingdom, which has otherwise, made no impression on our surnames.

The name **Flower**, itself, has a variety of origins: the producer of flour was one, but the word was sometimes given as a nickname to one (not necessarily a girl) possessing a sweet and agreeable nature or a delicate, petal-coloured complexion. By far the most frequently met flower name is **Rose** (**Royce** is an unexpected variant), as the London telephone directory shows: it tabulates 892 **Rose** entries and 23 of **Royce**. The rose sometimes appeared on inn signs and this may be a source of the name in some cases, recalling one who was employed at or who owned such an establishment. Scottish and Irish Gaelic, as well as Old German also offer their own roots of the name, as do two or three place-names which may have undergone a change of spelling in their transition to the surname. **Lilly** (and **Lilley**) also has mixed ancestry. It may have signified a white skin after the colour of the common flower (also catered for in the surname **Lillywhite**), or else it was gained by an émigré of the Hertfordshire village of **Lilley** (that is 'a flax field'). **Blanchflower**, an uncommon name nowadays, possibly did recall a pale complexion – rather unwelcome if applied to a young man, one would imagine.

There are one or two herb-names in current use as surnames, though these too, have origins other than the plants whose names they bear.

Sage derives from the Old French word for 'wise', a rather gratifying nickname, while **Dill** has a fearfully complicated set of possibilities, from a variant of **Dell**, through a development of 'dull', to a proposed (but not yet confirmed) derivative of a personal name Dylla.

I thought I'd briefly mention here the surname **Onions**, which occurs in small numbers nationwide. It may possibly originate in the French word *oignon*, an onion, and recall a seller of these vegetables, but its more likely origin is 'of Ennion'. A few bearers of the name prefer to adjust its form to **O'Nions**, in the hope of avoiding a direct association with the vegetable.

Finally, the surname **Plant** itself, represented a gardener, planter or the worker in the plantation.

In summary then, plants, other than trees, have made no real impression on our surnames from the point of view of physical characteristics, which is probably understandable. The only reasons a plant might have entered the nicknaming process would have been through its colour and when an individual had a taste for a particular edible plant.

So now we will pass from fauna and flora of the English countryside to the more abstract concept of time as a source of our surnames.

Nicknames from time and season

That such an abstract idea as time could have generated nicknames and ultimately surnames, is perhaps a little surprising. However, it has not been the concept itself of time, but the units of measurement of time that bear the responsibility in this case. Since there are many ways in which time is expressed, there is a large number of names to be found associated with the passage of time. If I begin with the names of months of the year, it might be an interesting introduction to glance at their frequency as current surnames as they appeared in the London telephone directory (though numerical changes are always taking place). Indeed, one might ask whether *all* of the months actually occur as surnames. Here is the London telephone directory list:

January	2	July	1
February	1	August	28
March	76	September	1
April	2	October	0
May	581	November	1
June	1	December	1

At the time of my survey, **October** seemed to be the odd-man-out with no entries at all in the London area, but the answer to the question

I posed as to whether *all* of the months appeared as surnames, is – yes they do, for there are currently 13 recorded individuals in the capital's electoral registers and 2 entries of the surname **October** in the Sheffield telephone directory.

March, **May**, and **August(e)** are outstanding in that they have a sizeable number of entries each: an indication that they may have alternative origins. This is in fact, the case. If we begin with these three months, we find that the surname **March** may have no connection with the third month in many cases, but may be a memory of a local feature name, that is, 'one who dwelt beside the boundary', or from a place-name (**March** in Cambridgeshire or Lanarkshire for example). **May**, the commonest of the twelve by a long way, is in large measure the Middle English word for 'a youth', as well as being a pet form of **Matthew**, evident in the surname **Mayhew**. Nevertheless, it is a rather pleasing thought that a child's birth during the pleasant and fragrant blossoming of the may perhaps inspired the name in some cases.

Two saints sharing the name Augustine (Latin, 'venerable, wise') prove to be the principal source of the surnames **August**, **Auguste**, **Argust**, **Austin** and **Austen**.

Of the remaining months, **February**, **September**, **November** and **December** must surely commemorate the time of birth of a child, while **January** may do so too, though it is also believed to be a corruption of **Janaway**, which was an Anglicised pronunciation of the Italian city of Genoa. Thus it may also be an expatriate's nickname. **April** is a rare surname today, as is its alternative French form **Averill** (though there is currently one of each in my local telephone book). This may also be recall the birth of a child, for **April** is the month of fresh awakening and new blossom, but is also a little unpredictable. As a forename, however, Avril is fairly recent. As for the months of **June** and **July**, the first perhaps owes more to the French 'jeune' ('young') than to the month of the child's birth, while the second, **July**, when not remembering the month of birth, is a contraction of the Latin personal name Julius.

So much for the twelve months of the year and their unusual contribution to our surnames. Despite their appearances **Weeks** and **Weekes** have nothing to do with the units of time, for they are variations of **Wicks**, from the Old English word 'wīc', which often indicated a special building such as a farm or even a small settlement. Their final '-s' gives them the appearance of plurals, but it almost certainly denotes a genitive, 'of'. They are clearly recalling a place-name or a local feature.

As for the days of the week themselves, only three of them occur in the London directories as surnames: **Monday** (2), **Tuesday** (2) and **Friday** (7) together with **Fryday** (2), though interestingly, the day-names in my local telephone book are **Friday** (3) and **Sunday** (3). **Monday** must have recalled the day of birth of a child, although it has now become inextricably confused with **Munday** and **Mundy**, which are from the Old Norse personal name Mundi ('protector'). **Tuesday** honours Tiw, the Teutonic god of war and will almost always recall the day of birth. Although **Thursday** (after Thor, the god of thunder) does not currently appear in the London book, I have tracked down one or two in other mainland telephone books, but it is very rare indeed now and will signify the child's day of birth. The name **Friday** commends the Norse goddess of love, Freyja. This day of the week was felt to be a day of ill-omen in the mediæval mind, being irrevocably bound to Christ's crucifixion and the season of Lent. A child born on Good Friday therefore, may have been named after this most important festival in spite of its undertones of gloom (hence the expression 'friday-face').

Saturday seems not to have survived into modern times and there is only a single instance of **Wednesday** in national electoral records.

Mention of the festival of Good Friday leads us to a consideration of other festivals and seasons of the year. **Spring**, **Summer**, **Winter**, **Midwinter**, **Easter**, **Christmas**, **Noel** and **Holiday** (that is, 'holy-day', when no work was done) are all represented in our surnames to a greater or lesser extent. There are several alternative spellings of **Holiday**: **Holliday** and **Halliday** are two of the most often seen and the nickname must have celebrated a birth on a holy day. All of these names can in fact, be explained in terms of seasonal births. In the case of Summer, however, Dr Reaney believes that there are no convincing grounds for ascribing the surname to the summer season, in spite of there being such names as **Winter** and **Spring** (though no Autumn). Instead, he favours a derivation from the French 'somier', a sumpter (one who looked after the pack-horses, often referred to as 'sumpters'). **Spring** is the time of re-birth, when Nature awakes and the idea of freshness and even nimbleness may have occasioned the nickname, rather than a direct reference to the actual season. **Winter**, however, may be a direct allusion to the season, particularly if a child were born in the depths of a severe one, although, being a gloomy time of the year, the name may also have been bestowed upon an older individual who rarely smiled or who had a naturally cheerless facial expression.

Easter is the most important of the Christian Church's festivals and a birth on Easter Day would have been auspicious enough to encourage parents to confer the nickname on the child. There are over 130 entries of the surname in the London electoral registers, so the name is in a relatively healthy state of survival. **Whitsun** is a contraction of 'White Sunday', when the newly baptised wore white robes. The birth on this festival day may be one origin or the surname. Another possible origin is borne in evidence to suggest that the nickname comes from 'White's son'. Indeed **Whiteson** exists as a surname, though an uncommon one (the London telephone directory has recently listed 6). Mediæval folk also knew Whitsuntide as **Pentecost** and a child born on this day would have naturally prompted such a nickname. The surname gallantly survives, with nearly a dozen showing in the London telephone directory.

Finally, the unusual name **Loveday** has an interesting origin. In the later middle ages, it became the custom to set aside an agreed day in order that parties engaged in a dispute or quarrel, might come together and seek a solution. Such a day was called a 'love-day' and any child born on this day might well have been given the name. In Old English, 'Leofdæg' was a well-used forename and this may also have assisted the survival of the surname.

Nicknames from coins and money

Improbable as it may seem, coins have been the generators of several interesting surnames. However, as we always seem to be finding in our investigation of the origins of surnames, things are not always as simple as they often first appear and those names that look straightforward in their meanings can have a surprise in store.

Those names which can definitely be ascribed to coins are **Halfpenny**, **Penny**, **Penney**, **Tuppenney** and **Shilling**. The simple expression of affection may be enough to account for such nicknames, though there may be other monetary reasons now forgotten. As a small child in the early 1950s, I can remember being called 'my little sixpunce' (sic), by a very old lady – so the idea may live yet. The only other coin which may possibly have had any relevance to our surnames is the **Noble,** a gold coin issued in 1344 by Edward III, the value of which was 6s 8d, that is, ⅓ of £1. Of course, the nickname may well have been acquired by one who had noble air or bearing, but it could also mean 'famous'. The most probable explanation for the nickname in most cases, however, lies in the mediæval pageants, which also produced names like **King** and **Pope**. There seems little reason to connect the name with the coin itself. A **Farthing** was one-quarter of a penny, though, as with the Noble, there is nothing really to associate the coin with the nickname. There are two possibilities for the origin of the name – the Old Norse 'Farthegn', a 'traveller' and the Old English 'feorthing', a fourth part' of a virgate of land (that is, about 30 acres). **Pound** may have referred to the maker of pound weights or to one who looked after the village pound, where straying animals were penned.

The surname **Coyne** recalls the die used in the stamping of coins and the term was probably used for the coiner or **Minter** of coins too. The surnames **Cash** and its variation **Cass** are really contractions of the women's personal name Cassandra, which is thought to be a feminine form of Alexander and which, though from the Greek, was a name in regular use during the middle ages.

An interesting surname which, however, bears no obvious clue as to its monetary origins is **Dismorr** (also **Dismore**). This name arose from the French 'dix mars'– 'ten marks' – a mark being equivalent to two nobles, or 13s 4d (that is ⅔ of £1). Just how it came to become a nickname is puzzling.

We now take our leave of coin nicknames with a pair of charming names which are still to be found, though rather rarely: **Fivepence** and **Twentypence**. Again, just how they became nicknames remains unclear. There are several other names in this pattern still to be seen occasionally.

Nicknames from games

Some activities must have been as obsessive to the mediæval Englishman as they are to his modern counterpart, especially gambling with dice. All levels of mediæval society were passionate about dicing and there were even dicing schools and gambling societies in the towns and cities. Women too, were often enthusiastic players. This aspect of gaming has made a direct impression on our surnames, as a quick check in the London telephone books will show – there are 6 entries of **Dice** and **Dyce**. A few other surnames have their origins in gaming nicknames: **Hazzard**, **Game**, **Chance**, **Gamester**, **Gammond**, and **Goodgame(s)** are some of them and fervent players would easily attract nicknames to themselves.

Recent London telephone books yield the following numbers for these surnames though, of course each edition is likely to list slight changes to the totals in each case:

Chance	45	Gamester	5
Game(s)	40	Gammond	5
Haz(z)ard	25	Goodgame(s)	2
Dice, Dyce	9		

Although the surname **Goodgame(s)** has only two entries in the London telephone directory, I count no fewer than 15 in the Oxford book, which must make this district a bastion of this interesting name.

Gamble would seem to offer no difficulties in interpretation, but here we have one of those cases of gentle deception, for the name has its origins in the Old Norse word 'gamal', meaning simply 'old'. **Player**, too looks a good candidate for this collection of names, but again we are deceived, for the name refers to a performer in plays and pageants.

Throwing games have always been popular, but they seem to have left no lasting impression on our surname inheritance: even **Thrower** was an occupational name for a thrower of clay pots or for one who prepared silk thread.

Nicknames from street cries and exclamations

Many of today's market traders shout their wares almost as lustily as their forebears must have done nine centuries ago, for there is no more effective and direct means of advertising one's merchandise and, as I pointed out in the section 'Nicknames from fish', such names as **Herring** and **Mullett** probably arose in this way. Traders would have bellowed their favourite phrases across the town and it is easy to see how these men earned appropriate nicknames. I have a clear memory of such an instance from my childhood: a pair of vegetable sellers, each getting on in years, slowly drove their waggon through the neighbourhood, one bawling what seemed to us children to be "Timorag!". Much later I learned that it was meant to be "Tomato!". We always called the crier Tim O'Rag and it was not until many years later that I found that his name was Arthur Cox!

Perhaps the most familiar surname which has its roots firmly in the ancient street cry category is **Goodall**, which is a metamorphosis of the cry, 'Good ale!' Whether their ale was 'good' was unlikely to have concerned the criers, for the brewers and alewives (the '**Brewsters**') hoped that their calls would bring along the customers, but would not attract attention from the civic ale-tasters, for the watering of ale was a common practice and was punishable by fine. The tasters, who could be women as well as men, were also on the look out for ale and wine that had gone sour. Dr Reaney[1] cites a Yorkshireman, who may have been a regular offender in this respect – William Sourale (1301) – for his name is more suggestive of an offender than of a drinker of sour ale! The name **Goodale** itself, has survived in small numbers (there are four in the London telephone directory), but is greatly out-numbered everywhere by **Goodall**. Another well known street call would have been 'Good beer!', which has turned itself, in some cases, into the name **Godber**. In other cases, the name is a compression of the expletive 'God be here!' It is a pity that so many of the known nicknames springing from mediæval street cries have faded away: Fresschbred ('Fresh bread!'), Swetmylk ('Sweet milk!') and Smalfis ('Small fish!')[2] are three examples that have all been recorded, but have long since been forgotten. Sadly, we have lost many colourful names.

Mention of the expletive, 'God be here!' leads us towards another group: those names whose origins lie in favourite and oft-repeated

---

1. P. H. Reaney (1979 edition) *The Origin of English Surnames.* Routledge & Keegan Paul.

2. Ibid.

phrases. Such phrases may have been expressions of anger, oaths, greetings, farewells or habitual utterances which crept unawares into a person's speech. They were the parallels of today's catchphrases, slogans and exclamations: 'Lumme!', ''Struth!', 'Wotcha!', 'Blimey!', 'Hey-up!' and dozens more. An example, in many ways analogous to these, is seen in the surname **Bygott**, 'By God!' and its French counterpart **Pardy**, 'par Dieu!' (with its variants **Pardoe** and **Pardew**)

A common greeting for many centuries has been 'good day', which has produced the surnames **Gooday** and **Goodey**, while sentiments of farewell and good hope for the future are embodied in **Goodyear** and **Goodier**. An uncommon name in this small, but interesting group, is **Goodspeed**, meaning 'God go with you' (it rates only 5 entries in the London telephone directory). Its French equivalent is **Dugard** ('Dieu garde', 'God protect you'), which is even less common than **Goodspeed**, having had only two instances in the London telephone directory in the last ten years. Perhaps we may also include **Benedict** here, coming straight from the Latin 'benedictus', 'blessed'.

Drinkall – 'drink ale' – may have amounted to a toast, or the nickname may have been given to one who usually drank more than was good for him. Similarly **Drinkdregs**, a most evocative name, emptied his mug down to the bottom, dregs and all, but what are we to make of **Drink-water**, a fairly common surname? One who preferred water to ale would be a most unlikely proposition, the populace being well aware of the dangers of drinking water from any source: wells, streams, rivers, pools or springs. It is very likely that the subject of such a nickname was a true lover of his ale and the nickname may be one of the many examples we have already noted of the Englishman's love of irony.

There aren't all that many surnames that come from street cries and expletives, but the few that we have inherited make an interesting little collection.

Nicknames from plays and pageants

Since almost all peasants and labouring citizens were illiterate and anyway, books of any kind were very scarce and highly valued by those who were well enough off to have them hand-copied, one way of teaching the masses was by the performance of plays and pageants. The various trade guilds would regularly present miracle and mystery plays which depicted Biblical stories and other moral ideas. These performances would often coincide with the arrival of itinerant fairs and were highly popular with all classes. The townsfolk of course, would have had many more opportunities to enjoy such occasions than their country cousins who, for the most part, had to be content with pictures in coloured glass windows (if the village church were fortunate enough to have been endowed with such a luxury) and wall paintings, while the parson taught them Biblical stories and said Latin prayers. City-dwellers were, by comparison to the rural population, better educated, or at least they enjoyed the opportunities of more varied experiences and contact with visitors from outside the community.

The characters in the plays were many and varied and the parts were regularly played by the same actors who inevitably became associated with their characters in the minds of the spectators. Thus we have an explanation for such surnames as **King** and **Pope**, since the names could hardly have derived from the actual holders of such exalted offices. The same must also be true of **Prince**, **Duke**, **Earl** (**Hearle** and **Hurl** are variations of this name), **Barron**, **Knight**, **Abbott** and **Bishop** (but for more on **Bishop**, see Chapter Two, The Church). It's pretty clear that all of these names represent male offices for, apart from the king's wife and some of the wives of high-ranking noblemen who nevertheless, held no official power, women were denied offices of state and the highest executive station a woman might achieve was abbess of a nunnery.

The surname **Player** seems also to have originated in the mystery plays and describes the general performer. Many Biblical characters became familiar to the population by way of the plays and pageants, as well as through the teachings of the parson and friars. The Bible, as we should have expected, has furnished us with not only many forenames, but many surnames too (see Chapter Eight).

The booming voice of God was often to be heard in plays and the actor taking this role must have become closely associated with the part. However, this was forbidden ground as far as nicknaming went and the nearest approach permissible was **Good**. On the other hand, the devil *has* crept into our names, presenting himself in such terms as **De Ville**, **Devall**, **Deval** and so forth. Certain deft changes of spelling and shape of the word help to make it less obvious that we are encountering a mediæval pageant player, though such modifications only just manage to conceal the actual sound of the original word (compare the names having the suffix '-bottom' in Chapter Four, Surnames from Local Features). Perhaps the town of Deville in Ardennes in Northern France offers a welcome escape route from a somewhat discouraging surname origin.

The symbolism of **Death** had a powerful influence on all ranks and classes of society and it is hardly surprising that the word became a nickname for the player of the part, who probably relished his role. Following my observations on the transformations of the word 'devil' in the last paragraph, we will not be very surprised to find that subsequent bearers of the name **Death** have also tried to disguise its dark origin by re-shaping it as **D'Eath** and **De Ath**, thus diverting attention towards the

Belgian town of **Ath**. I have also recently heard the name pronounced 'Deeth'.

The rather abstract names **Peace**, **Hope**, **Wisdom** and **Faith** can also trace their origins to the allegorical mediæval plays, **Hope** having become the most frequently occurring of the group (see also 'Abstract nicknames' earlier in this chapter).

A Nickname Postscript

I thought I would end this long chapter on nicknames with a few that are colourful, unusual and evocative, but which do not otherwise belong together. The charming name **Boughtflower** really does exist – there are approaching 30 bearers in the London districts (and my local telephone book lists a single entry). Although it may sound like a complete invention, it meant 'bolted (milled) flour' and must have been the miller's or flour grinder's nickname in some localities.

Scattergood, a surname occurring mostly in the north of England, though there is 1 currently in my local telephone book, is one of those names that could have contradictory meanings. It may have meant exactly what it says when applied to a generous and charitable friend to the poor, or it may have been used in an ironical way when applied to an habitual, miserable skinflint.

The Norman word 'cachepol' 'chase fowl', is the source of the common English surname **Catchpole** and recalls the court officer whose duty was to collect debts and to deliver warrants on the court's behalf.

Eatwell sounds as though we are faced with an ancestor of outstanding appetite, but the name almost certainly arises from the individual whose home village had been Etwell in Derbyshire. **Lickorish** (also **Lickerish** and **Liquorish**) may seem an unlikely surname, but the dozen or so London electoral entries prove that it is a survivor. It springs from the Middle English word 'likerous', 'lecherous or wanton', a rather surprising survivor! If **Lickorish** is not at all what it seemed, then neither is **Custard**. This is a variation of **Costard**, which is the old English word for an apple and may have been given to the apple seller, or else it was used in a slightly derogatory way to describe one with an apple-shaped head (compare **Perrett** – 'pear-shaped head').

Smoker and **Spittle** are unusual, but not altogether rare (the London districts' electoral registers list 28 and 77 entries respectively) and in juxtaposition, they seem to have a rather disagreeable kinship. However, illusion is again at work here, for **Smoker** meant 'smocker', the maker of the smocks worn by many labourers and **Spittle** (**Spittal** too) derives from the attendant at the mediæval 'hospital'.

A close look at **Wagstaffe** and **Shakespeare** will reveal a similarity of meaning. They may well have indicated a certain skill with the spear or the quarterstaff, but our mediæval ancestors were quite ready to apply such suggestive words in a purely sexual context. The same explanations may be true of **Longstaffe**.

Bearers of the surname **Lovelady** must all have endured a good deal of tiresome folly through the ages and I'm afraid that its history offers little comfort. It was undoubtedly given to one who indeed, had an eye for a little feminine charm and was akin to receiving the nickname **Spendlove** (in its literal origin). I have already mentioned a more sinister origin of **Spendlove** in the section *'Three grim nicknames'* earlier in this chapter. **Loveman** also exists (about 70 show up in the national electoral records, though the London districts record only 9). It may have been applied to one of either gender.

Of course, there are hundreds of these interesting and colourful names to be found and a glance through any local telephone book will turn up plenty of them. They are well worth a study in themselves, but we must not forget that things are frequently not what they seem at first, as **Silly** and **Batty** will find![1]

---

1. See the foot of page 144.

Chapter 8

Surnames from Personal Names

Old English personal names

And so we have reached the last of our surname groups – those that have their roots in ancient personal names. We have seen that most English surnames have their origins in the years following the Norman Conquest and indeed, very many of them are based on words, place-names and personal names brought from France by the victorious Norman invaders. However, there are still many names in use today whose histories reach back well before the Norman invasion of 1066. The pre-Conquest Briton had no fixed secondary name, nor did he need one, for communities were small and almost entirely rural, town life being generally distasteful to native inhabitants. Each individual in a settlement was known to every other by his or her personal name, which sometimes must have been displaced by a nickname which drew attention to some handicap or an unusual physical or behavioural feature, though we have little recorded evidence of this. Nicknames deriving from occupations or localities, however, were to be a predominantly post-Conquest phenomenon, although Dr Reaney[1] has uncovered a recorded example of an occupational sobriquet nearly a century before Duke William's intervention into Britain's affairs, in one Ecceard Smið (the smith).

On many occasions throughout this book, I have referred to Old English words and names as progenitors of many of our surnames, so these too constitute a very important source in our study of the descent of our names. Old English personal names were sometimes simple like Hwita and Leofa, though it was a custom to combine one element of the father's name with one element of the mother's name when naming a newborn child (see Chapter Seven, *Nicknames from animals*, for more on this). This idea undoubtedly went far towards the establishment of a close bond between the child and each of its parents, though the process allows only a limited number to be compounded before repetition. The process must also result in the formation of many literally senseless

1. P. H. Reaney (1976) *A Dictionary of British Surnames*. Routledge & Keegan Paul.

names, such as Wulfstan ('wolf-stone') and Ælfread ('elf-council'). The fact that the compounds were literal nonsense was of no importance to the 10th and 11th century Englishmen: they had succeeded in their purpose of forging a name-bond between themselves and their offspring and of evoking a special mystical spirit within the growing child.

From the end of the 10th century, the simple type of personal name became used less often and parents increasingly formed their children's names from a handful of familiar elements. By doing so, the name-bond tradition between the parent and the child was lost. Some of the commonly used first elements were:

Ælf	'elf';	God	'God' or 'good';
Æthel	'noble';	Leof	'beloved';
Beorht	'bright';	Sig	'victory';
Ead	'prosperity';	Wulf	'wolf'.
Frith	'peace';		

These first elements were then combined with a number of endings, some of which are :

-eald	'old';	-stan	'stone';
-gifu	'gift';	-weard	'protector';
-hild	'war';	-wig	'warrior' or 'war';
-mund	'guardian';	-wine	'friend';
-ræd	'council';	-wulf	'wolf'.
-ric	'ruler';		

As I said, these are not the only elements from which the Britons were able to form their personal names, but they are the ones that we see most frequently and a large number of combinations was possible (in theory, 98 are possible from those listed above, not counting 'Wulfwulf', of course).

The group in the list to follow includes some combinations whose meanings make acceptable sense, as well as some that do not and I have added the modern surnames which have evolved from each personal-name combination:

Æthelwine ('noble friend')	– **Alwin**;
Eadmund ('prosperity guardian')	– **Edmund(s)**, **Edmond(s)**;
Ealfric ('elf-ruler')	– **Eldridge**, **Aldridge**, **Aldrich**;
Godric ('god-friend')	– **Goodrich**;
Godwine ('god-friend')	– **Godwin**, **Goodwin**;
Leofric ('beloved leader')	– **Loveridge**;
Leofwine ('beloved friend')	– **Lewin**;

Wigmund ('warrior-protector')	– **Wyman**;
Wulfric ('wolf-ruler')	– **Woolrich**, **Wooldridge**;
Wulfsig ('wolf-victory')	– **Wolsey**.

Although these compound personal names have provided the foundations of many of our surnames, the simple, uncompounded personal names which I mentioned earlier in this section, have also contributed their share to the process. It is not always easy, however, to assign a distinct meaning to them. Here are ten of them, together with the surname we know today:

Bynni ('a manger', or 'hollow')	– **Binns**;
Ceadda	– **Chad**, **Chadd**;
Clac (possibly a nickname for a chatterbox)	– **Clack**;
Creoda	– **Creed**;
Dodda or Dudda	– **Dodd**, **Dodds**;
Cene or Cyne ('wise' or 'brave')	– **Keen**;
Pymma	– **Pimm**, **Pym**;
Snel ('bold', 'active')	– **Snell**;
Tat	– **Tate**;
Wada	– **Wade** (a tale of a sea giant called Wade has probably helped to preserve this name. It may also refer to a ford).

Looking at these original Old English personal names, their very unfamiliarity makes us feel very distant indeed from our past, but through our surnames, they do give us a slender bond with those fascinating and enigmatic Britons who lived in these islands over a millennium ago.

Biblical names

Augustine, a Benedictine prior from Rome, arrived on the shores of Kent in AD597, having been sent by Pope Gregory to lead a mission to the court of King Æthelberht I, with the goal of converting the pagan English king to Christianity. On Christmas Day of that year the King was indeed converted and received baptism. Augustine became the first Archbishop of Canterbury in AD598 and gradually, through his teaching, the names of the Apostles and other Biblical people became known to many of the islanders, beginning with the Kentish folk.

By the beginning of the 13th century, every peasant and citizen would have been familiar with the stories and the names of the Apostles, the doings and sayings of the great Biblical characters, as well as the lives of the saints. It may seem surprising therefore, that over the five centuries since Augustine's mission, so few of the Biblical personal names had been adopted by Englishmen. The truth of this is to be seen in Domesday. This great register of land values and property was completed in 1087 and contains hundreds of typically Saxon names like Wulfwy, Alwin, Godwin, Segrim and Ælfeva. Unfortunately for us, only the important landholders are named and we are told only the *numbers* of peasants in each village:

"Godfrey holds Holton from Roger. 5 hides. Land for 7 ploughs. Now in lordship 2 ploughs; 4 slaves. 10 villagers with 3 smallholders have 4 ploughs. Meadow, 15 acres; pasture, 12 acres; woodland 2 furlongs Long and 1½ furlongs wide. The value is and was £4."

– Translated from the Domesday entry for the village of Holton near Oxford.

If only we could know the names of the seventeen peasants working the Holton land! There can be little doubt that mostly, they and their wives and children would have had traditional English names, for twenty years of Norman domination could not have been enough to have altered traditions extending back several hundred years. However, King William's object in commissioning the preparation of Domesday was not at all of a social nature, as is the case with our modern census objectives, but had a purely fiscal and military intention.

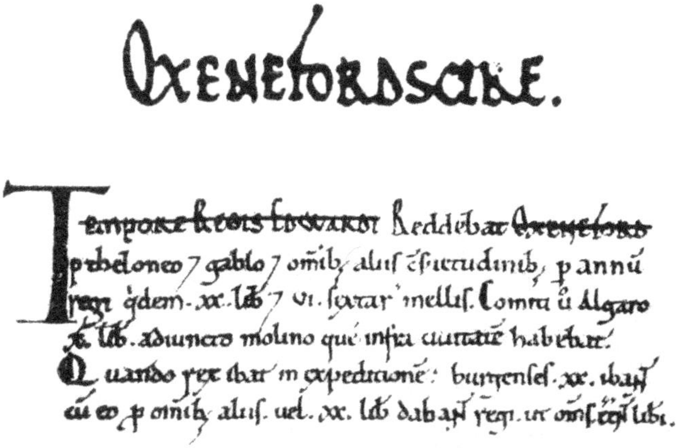

Figure 2. The beginning of the Domesday entry for Oxfordshire.

Biblical names are not completely absent, however, and we do come across the occasional Adam, Joseph, Peter, Solomon and Matthew. With the coming of the Normans, however, came a steady spread across England of Biblical personal names, so that by the end of the 13th century, pre-Conquest English names had largely fallen out of favour. Most names we see in the records of the time are of Norman or Biblical origin. This can be explained in the first instance, by the native population's growing awareness of the Norman landholders and their families, together with the Norman officials, with whom the peasantry became gradually familiar. Town dwellers, especially in the south and south-east, were to feel the attraction of the new names sooner than their country fellows, through such events as the coronations of the monarchs, the murder of Thomas Becket in Canterbury in 1170 and the growing trade with foreigners from the near Continent.

It was the Conqueror's grandson, Stephen, who was to be the first English monarch to bear a Biblical forename, named after the first Christian martyr. That King Stephen's name did not become a popular one is perhaps due in part, to his disastrous reign ("...the 19 long winters ..." of civil strife and lawlessness, 1135-1154). Fifty years after Stephen, we find another unpopular king bearing another New Testament name – John – a name that was already becoming well used throughout England. The Apostle John was called the favourite of Jesus and was the closest to the Messiah of all His followers, a fact that may have inspired the popularity of the name. By the early 14th century, John had become the most common forename in the kingdom, surpassing even William and Robert in popularity.

The original Apostles were **Andrew**, **Bartholomew**, **James** (two men had this name**)**, **John**, **Jude** (also known as Thaddeus), **Matthew**, **Philip**, **Simon**, **Peter** (who was originally Simon, but was re-named by Jesus), **Thomas** and Judas. After Judas's suicide, his place was taken by **Matthias** and later **Paul** was included too.

The name Judas (the Greek form of Jude) understandably gained no support at all of course; no one would wish their child to be associated with the betrayer of the Messiah, even after a thousand years. The name might otherwise have become well adopted, since one of Jesus' half-brothers was also called Judas. The name **Jude**, too, may have proved too close to the sound of Judas to have gained much ground in the surname stakes. The following list, taken from recent London telephone directories, gives an interesting comparison of the modern-day popularity of the surnames derived from the names of the Apostles.

The '-s' ending, where it denotes relationship, increases the incidence of all but two, up to twenty times:

		James	1680
		Jude	19
		Matthias	14
		Thomas	2461
Andrew	45	Andrews	855
Bartholomew, Bate	142	Bates	311
John	325	Johns	189
Matthew, Mayhew	166	Matthews	75
Paul, Paull	401	Pauls	2
Peter	37	Peters	490
Philip, Phillip	93	Philips, Phillips	1932
Simon	205	Simons, Simmon(d)s	1005
TOTAL	1414	TOTAL	5659

Jude and **Matthias** are the least common surnames today, while **Paul** may well be hidden in names like **Poll**, **Pole** and even **Powell**. There are many variations, contractions, modifications and compounds of the Apostles' names, as we might expect:

Bartholomew (Hebrew, 'son of Talmai'); **Bate, Batey, Bates, Barth, Bartle, Bartlett, Bateman, Bateson, Bartleman**.

Andrew (Greek, 'manly'); **Andros, Andre, Andress, Anders, Anderson, Andresson, Andrews, Mastrandrea**.

John (Hebrew, 'whom Yahwey has favoured'); **Jenks, Jenkins, Junkin, Hankin**, plus about another dozen.

Matthew (Hebrew, 'gift of God'); **Mayhew, May, Makin, Matt, Mathis, Matthews. Matthew**, as a personal name, is one of the few Biblical names to appear in any numbers in Domesday.

Philip (Greek, 'lover of horses'); **Phelps, Phipps, Philpott(s), Pipkin, Phillips, Philipson**.

Simon ('Greek, 'snub-nosed'). There are several dozen variations and derivatives of this name, of which the following is a selection: **Sim, Simms, Simmond(s), Simson, Simpson, Simmonite, Simkin, Simpkin**.

James (a form of **Jacob**. Hebrew, 'one who takes by the heel' – i.e. one who overthrows another); **Jameson, Jamison, Jacques, Jacks, Jackson, Jempson** and several others.

Thomas (Aramaic, 'a twin'); **Tomms, Thomson, Thompson, Thomasson, Tomlin, Tomlinson, Tomkins, Tompkins, Tonks**. Various others.

Other New Testament names that have been adopted as surnames, or as the bases of surnames are:

Mark and **Marks** (from Mars, the Roman god of War). Mark was Paul's companion and the traditional author of the Second Gospel. The name, however, was not widely favoured in mediæval times.

Barnabas (Hebrew, 'son of consolation'). Barnabas was the cousin of Mark and his name has produced **Barnaby** and **Barney**. It has never been a common surname.

Luke (one from Lucania in Southern Italy); **Lukes, Luker, Luck, Luckett, Lucas**.

Joseph (Mary's husband. Hebrew, 'Jehovah adds'); a man generally held in some affection, but at the same time, possessing an air of mystery;

Josephs, Josephson, Jessop (where the two vowels have become transposed; possibly the result of a mispronunciation of the Italian Giuseppe).

The River Jordan too, has been the source of a common name: **Jordan** and its shorter versions **Judd** and **Jurd**. This name may have found its way to Britain via the Crusaders returning from the Holy Land wars in the 11th, 12th and 13th centuries.

Turning now to the Old Testament, we find a profusion of personal names that have become surnames and almost all of them are from men's personal names. There are relatively few which derive from women's names:

Eve (Hebrew, 'life'); **Evett** ('little Eve'), **Evison** ('son of Eve'),

Evins ('of little Eve'), **Eva, Everson**. There are variations of spelling for several of these, but even so, they do not occur as surnames in great numbers.

Sarahs (Hebrew, 'princess'); 'of Sarah'. A rare surname nowadays.

Susans (a shortened form of the Hebrew Susanna, 'a lily'); 'of Susannah'. Also a rarely seen surname today.

Mary: a very rare surname today, but see Chapter Five for the many names derived from this.

In general, Biblical women's names were not widely adopted by the mediæval English.

Two of the most frequently encountered Biblical names in our surnames are **Adam** (Hebrew, 'red') and **David** (Hebrew, possibly 'beloved' or 'chieftain'). They appear in a number of simple variations: **Adams, Adkin, Aitken, Aitkin, Adcock, Davids, Davey, Davy, Davis, Davies** and **Davys**. The London telephone books list 1194 entries of **Adam** and **Adams** and 4787 of **David**, together with its six variations mentioned above.

Two other respected Old Testament names are **Abraham** (Hebrew, 'father of the multitude') and **Isaac** (Hebrew, 'laughter'). The story of this father and son pair would have made a deep impression on the minds of the parsons' mediæval gatherings, on account of the absolute devotion to God's will on the part of the father and the innocence and trust on the part of the son. The two names are not necessarily indicators of Jewish ancestry. The current London telephone directory records 376 instances of **Abraham** and **Abrahams** and 268 of **Isaac** and **Isaacs**.

The two sons of Adam and Eve were **Cain** (Hebrew, 'a spear') and **Abel** (Hebrew, 'a breath'). Although variations on the name **Cain** are not rare (**Cane**, **Kain**, **Kaine** and **Kayne** are some), they will often have originated either from a mediæval expatriate of the French town of Caen, or from the Welsh Gaelic word meaning 'beautiful'. As with the name Judas, it seems unlikely that parents would wish to name sons after an infamous murderer of his brother and use of the name would anyway, be strongly discouraged by the preachers and parsons of the locality. Cain's younger brother, **Abel**, however, found favour with God we are told, a fact that may well have encouraged the adoption of the name (which means 'son' in the Assyrian language).

The hero **Daniel** (Hebrew, 'God has judged') has made a worthy contribution to our surnames, as the 545 London telephone books' entries of **Daniel** and **Daniels** prove.

Other Old Testament personal names that have become surnames are usually found in relatively small numbers in our telephone books and electoral registers. Nevertheless, they are still worth looking at. Here are some of them:

Elias (the Greek form of Hebrew Elijah, 'The Lord is God');

Ezra (Hebrew, 'help');

Gabriel (Hebrew 'God is strong'); **Gabriele**;

Joshua (Hebrew, 'God is salvation');

Moses (possibly Hebrew, though of uncertain meaning); **Moss, Mosson, Mossman**;

Samson (Hebrew, 'sun'); **Sampson, Sansom**;

Samuel (Hebrew, 'asked of God'); **Samuels, Samwell**;

Saul (Hebrew, 'asked for');

Solomon (Hebrew 'shalom', 'peace'); **Salomon, Salmon, Sammond**,

Sammonds, Sammons. It is interesting that one the 20th century's greatest pianists, an Englishman, was always known only by the name of **Solomon**. His surname was **Cutner**.

This chapter has shown how important many Biblical personal names became during the critical mediæval period of surname formation, which is hardly surprising when one remembers that the Bible was a major source of stories and lessons for the English population, almost all of whom could not read. The great impression made on the receptive minds of peasants and citizens of the almost mythical characters is reflected in the upsurge of Biblical names, though they are almost all names of men.

Surnames from Saints' names

Apart from the Apostles' names just discussed, we have inherited a sizable number of names from the saints. Many have come from the Roman Empire and have both Latin and Greek origins, while others are descended from northern European lands.

During the middle ages, many guilds of craftsmen, trades and other bodies adopted appropriate saints as their patrons and holy protectors. Perhaps because these saints had been exceptionally pious humans, their names and spirits could be invoked as witnesses and comforters in moments of human weakness and distress without fear of blasphemy and it was felt that, in return for sincere reverence, the spirit of the saint would grant protection and prosperity to the company. The saints represented sublime examples of the utmost devotion a human being could exhibit and it is not at all surprising that many of their names have appeared as both forenames and ultimately, surnames. Indeed, the name **Saint** itself, first recorded in a mid-13th century document, may have reflected one having a truly pious nature, or else the reverse – one who only pretended to be devout and godly. In a few surnames, the word 'saint' has been retained, but in a shortened form ('Sin-' or 'St') as a prefix to the personal name. Examples of this in common usage are **Sinclair** (Saint Claire) and **StJohn** (pronounced 'Sinjen'). There are two places in France called St Clair, which undoubtedly also contribute to the origin of the surname, as well as several saints who bear the name. **St John** usually refers to St John the Baptist and meant 'one whom God has favoured'.

Out of the many saints current in mediæval times, I have chosen 25 who have contributed something significant, or at least interesting, to our surname heritage. Although there have been many women saints, I have included only four of them here; the names of others, together with their derivatives arose in Chapter Five. The small number of entries in the London telephone directory emphasises the already well-proven fact that women's personal names have made only a minor contribution to the evolution of our surnames. The numbers in brackets refer to the entries in the London telephone books at the time of my research.

Agatha (Greek, 'good'). This is the name of a pre-6th century saint who was martyred after torture. Her name is found in the occasional surnames **Agace** (1) and **Agass** (16).

Agnes (Greek, 'pure'); she was martyred by the sword in Rome at the age of 13 in about the year AD350. There was a widespread cult in her name from early times. The name appears as **Agness** (2), **Annis** (90) and the diminutive **Aggett** (4).

Adrian (13) and **Adrien** (3), meaning 'one from the Adriatic', is a common enough first name, but a much less common surname, which is a little curious since the only Englishman ever to have become Pope

– Nicholas **Breakspear** – held the office from 1154 to 1159, an important time in the surname-forming period. His was a short tenure it is true, but significantly, he assumed the appellation Adrian IV. He was never canonised 'saint', however. The actual St Adrian was, for several centuries, the chief military saint of Northern Europe and was regarded as the patron saint of old soldiers and protector against the plague.

Alban (3) and **Albin** (4) meant 'of Alba', an ancient Italian city. St Alban was the first English martyr. He was a soldier who was converted to Christianity by a priest whom he had protected from a mob. He was later beheaded by order of Rome in the early 4th century, at a place traditionally believed to be on the site now occupied by St Alban's cathedral in Hertfordshire.

Ambrose (102) (Greek, 'immortal'). Ambrose was a 4th century bishop of Milan and renowned as a preacher having, and demanding exacting standards of devotion. He was also the author of two volumes of hymns and religious discourses. He is the patron saint of bee-keepers and candle makers.

Anne (Hebrew, 'Hannah', 'grace') was the mother of the Virgin Mary. The surname **Hannah** (47) is the most frequent form of this name, while **Ann** (2) occurs only rarely. **Anns** (4) is the possessive form (i.e. 'of Ann') and **Annett** (23) is the most common diminutive.

Benedict (13) comes from the Latin 'benedictus', meaning 'blessed'. St Benedict was a 6th century Italian saint and is regarded as the father of western monasticism. **Bennett** (1424), the diminutive form ('little Benedict') is a very common form of this saint's name.

Bernard (135) (Old German 'bear-brave') was a 12th century abbot of Clairvaux in north-east France and is said to have inspired the First Crusade (1096-99), by which act he probably increased the popularity of the name, which was already in use as a personal name before Domesday (AD1086-87). The surname is found more often today as **Barnard** (2570) and **Barnett** (560), though this is also a place-name.

Brice (69) and **Bryce** (44), is a Celtic personal name of uncertain meaning. St Bricius was a bishop of the French town of Tours during the 5th century. The name became firmly established during the 12th and 13th centuries. However, **Brice** and **Price** are also contractions and variations of the Welsh 'Ap **Rhys**', meaning 'son of Rhys'.

Clement (67) (Latin, 'mild'). St Clement had been a friend and disciple of St Paul and subsequently became Pope Cement I and Bishop of Rome. He was imprisoned by the Emperor Trajan and eventually executed at the end of the 1st century. The name has given rise to more than a dozen variants, including **Clemmens** (23), **Clemmence** (12) and **Clements** (307). St Clement was the patron saint of tanners.

Denis (13), the French version of the Greek name Dionysus (the god of wine). **Denis** is the name of a number of saints, the principal one being a 3rd century Bishop of Paris. His success as a converter of pagans to Christianity led to his execution by outraged pagan priests. He was later adopted as the patron saint of France. The surname is much more common in the form **Dennis** (284).

Edmund(s) (83) is an Old English personal name, 'prosperity-protector'. This is the name of two saints and three English kings, the earliest of whom was also a saint. This king-saint was king of East Anglia during the 9th century and was killed by the occupying Danes. He was buried at Bury St Edmunds. The later saint, by the name of Edmund Rich (died 1240) was an Archbishop of Canterbury. The name has become one of the most frequently used non-Biblical saints' names, especially in the forms **Edmond** and **Edmonds** (146).

Francis (869), from the Latin 'Franciscus', 'a Frenchman'. The surname must have received some stimulus from the cult that arose following the arrival in England of the Franciscan friars in 1224. St Francis of Assisi (1181-1226), described as 'the little poor man' and '…the most blameless and gentle of all saints', founded the Franciscan order of Grey Friars. As recently as 1980 St Francis has been proclaimed the patron saint of ecology. **Franks** (156) is another common form of his name.

Gervais (6) (Latin, Gervaisius, of uncertain meaning, but perhaps 'spear-servant'). Rather an obscure person, St Gervase and his twin brother were beaten to death in mid-2nd century Milan. His remains are said to have worked miracles long after his death. The name is found most often as **Jarvis** (399) and **Jervis** (29).

Gregory (476) (Greek, 'watchful'). There were two saints of this name, both of whom were Popes. The earlier, 6th century saint (Gregory the Great), was responsible for St Augustine's mission to Britain in 596-7 to begin the task of converting Britons to Christianity. The later St Gregory was an 8th century Pope. Several of our surnames recall these saints: **Gregg**, **Grigg**, **Gregson** and **McGreggor** are some of them.

England's own patron saint, **George** (571) (Greek, 'farmer') was not a native of the British Isles, but is believed to have been born in Cappadocia – modern Turkey – in the late 3rd century. There is no firm evidence of his existence, however. The legend tells of his eventual execution. He is the patron saint of several other countries, including Ethiopia, Greece and Portugal. There are not many variations of his name: **Georges** (5), **Gorge** (3) and **Georgeson** (4) are the ones most likely to be encountered.

Giles (274), from the Greek for 'a kid', was a 6th or 7th century native of Athens and has long been the patron saint of cripples and beggars. Little is known of his life, however.

If we measure the popularity by surname variation and frequency, there can have been few martyrs more popular than was St **Laurence**. The name meant simply 'from Laurentium', an Italian town. According to tradition, this 3rd century saint was martyred by roasting on a gridiron, a fate which led to his being adopted as the patron saint of cooks. The more usual form of his name is **Lawrence** (1090), but it has a number of derivatives which include **Lawrie, Lourie, Lorenz, Lawson** and **Lowson**.

Leger (8) (Germanic, 'people-spear') recalls a 7th century French Bishop of Autun who suffered agonising torture and martyrdom in about AD679. **Ledger** (39) is the more common spelling of the surname.

Helen (Greek, Helena, 'bright'). St Helena was the wife of a 4th century Roman general and mother of the Roman Emperor **Constantine**. She lived a quiet life, giving much service to the poor. Helen's supposed discovery of the relics of Christ's execution cross has prompted her adoption as the patron saint of archæologists. She was not martyred, but by mediæval times, several monasteries observed her feast day. Her name gives rise to several fairly uncommon surnames like **Ellinor** (1), **Ellens** (3), **Hellens** (17) and the diminutive **Ellett** (10).

Michael (318) is the Greek form of a Hebrew word meaning 'who is like God'. Several Biblical individuals bore this name, but the most important source of the surname was the New Testament archangel and chief of the angels. We most often meet the surname in a form derived from the French, **Mitchell** (1475). However, a complication arises here in that **Mitchell** may also have roots in the Old English word 'mycel', meaning 'big', which has produced the name **Meikle**. We occasionally come across the transformations **Miell** and **Myhill** too.

Over two thousand **Martin**s are listed in the London telephone book, confirming that this surname is the most common surname derived from a non-Biblical saint. He was born in AD316, the son of an officer in the Roman army. Eventually he became Bishop of Tours in France and helped found early western monasticism. He is remembered best for his act of sharing his wine with a beggar at a feast, an act which undoubtedly led to his being chosen as the patron saint of lovers of alcohol. The name **Martin** itself, is a diminutive of the personal name Mars, the Roman god of war and implies 'little Mars'. It was a personal name only occasionally in use during the middle ages.

Patrick (96) (Latin 'patricius', 'noble man') was a 5th century British-born missionary who became Ireland's patron saint. His name has produced many variations, like **Patt, Pate, Patey, Paton, Petrie** and **Patterson**. The surname **Patrick** itself, was more often found in Scotland until the 17th century, when its use in Ireland began to increase.

The name **Valentine** (108) (Latin, 'valere', 'to be strong') probably owes its origin to a 3rd century Roman saint, though there were several others of this name. His connection with lovers' pursuits is an accident of the calendar. The festival of St Valentine was traditionally 14th February. On the following day, boys would draw the names of girls from a 'love-urn' in celebration of the beginning of the annual Roman fertility festival. Rather than abolish this festival, Pope Gelasius decided to move it back a day to coincide with the festival of St Valentine. Thus lovers have long since chosen St Valentine as their patron saint.

An early Spanish martyr gives our final name in this chapter: **Vincent** (297), from the Latin 'vincere', to conquer. **Vincent** was tortured and executed by the Roman Emperor Diocletian at the beginning of the 4th century for refusing to deny his Christian beliefs. The same name was borne, however, by several other early saints and appears in documents of the 13th century. It is a common surname together with a couple of variants: **Vincett** and **Vinson.**

In total, there are several thousand saints named in the Catholic archives and, glancing quickly through the lists one can pick out many names that are recognisable surnames today: **Burkard**, **Fursey**, **Myron**, **Osmund**, **Sylvester**, **Terence**, and **Victor**, as randomly picked examples, are all well represented in our surnames and all are worth personal investigation.

Very nearly every day of the year is a saint's day and some days are associated with several saints, celebrating saints from the earliest Christian years to much more recent ones. As with the Biblical names in the previous section, the almost superhuman goodness and strength of the saints caught the mediæval imagination and thus began the steady penetration of their names into early surnames (and personal names).

Postscript

Over these eight chapters I have covered only about two percent of British surnames in use today. Although much work has been done by scholars of this subject since William Camden's day (his book 'Britannia', containing his work on surnames, was first published in the 1680s) there is clearly a great deal left to do. Perhaps only a quarter of the possible 100,000 British surnames have been investigated so far, so there is plenty of scope for further research. Interest in surnames often begins with a desire to know something of one's family history, a subject which has increased in popularity over the last few decades, especially so since the advent of the Internet, and since we are likely to encounter at least 32 different surnames (mathematically 2^5 – that is, 2 x 2 x 2 x 2 x 2) if we look back only five generations and conceivably 1024 (2^{10}) at the tenth generation, it is surely worth getting to know something of their histories and meanings. It is for this very reason that I have written this book. Although it is only an introduction to the subject, I hope it may have served to sharpen your appetite and perhaps encourage you to look into your family's history, with special attention to the surnames encountered along the way. After all, it is through our forebears' surnames that we are able to trace the threads of our descent.

It is amazing to realise that the Norman Conquest of England occurred only about 31 generations ago (taking thirty years as one generation) and that within about fourteen generations of that event, surnames had become almost universal and hereditary in England. Only five generations later, their spellings too, had become fixed in most cases.

It seems to me that we generally take too little interest in our surnames and their histories, probably because of their very familiarity to us. This is rather a pity because, after all, as I said at the very beginning of the book, they are our most personal possession (next to our life itself), with which we can do as we like: we can alter their spellings, add more names to them, subtract from them, abandon them for other names or just drop them altogether; no one can stop us. But we all still feel the need for them, and not only for ourselves. As I said earlier, we name our pets, houses, farms, villages, garden roses, schools, pubs, dolls, teddy bears and even our motorcars. Names have become such a fundamental element in our existence that to remain ignorant of all that they can teach us must leave us the poorer in our understanding of our past.

One of the marvels of our surnames is that they give us an insight into our mediæval forebears' thinking, their habits and attitudes, their work and their play.

I leave you with a short list of particularly interesting and colourful surnames which I have seen recently. A few speak for themselves, some are not what they seem and the rest will need a little more investigation, but they all offer a glimpse of the fascinating diversity that is to be found in our surnames:

Andrejew, Andrewartha, Bensusan, Boffin, Claff, Doubtfire, Fairservice, Goodluck, Grindrod, Heaven, Henbest, Hollobone, Pepperdine, Possee, Prytherch, Quarshie, Raghip, Singmaster, Smartwest, Snailum, Stananought, Stelfox, Sweetapple, Wiblin, Wogman, Woodiwiss.

* From page 129: **Silly** is a variation of **Sealey**, from the Old English 'sælig' and meant 'blessed'. **Batty** is simply a pet form of **Bartholomew**.

Bibliography

Addison, Sir W. A. 1978 edition *Understanding English Surnames*. Batsford.

Anon. *Domesday Book (1086-87)*.

Bagley, J. J. 1971 *Life In Mediæval England*. Batsford.

Bardsley, Canon C. W. 1978 edition *English Surnames*. Batsford.

Beresford, M. 1971 *Deserted Mediæval Villages*. Cambridge University Press, Cambridge.

B.T. *Mainland telephone directories*.

Camden, W. 1870 edition *Remains Concerning Britain*. John Russell Smith.

Chaucer, Geoffrey. Late 14th century. *Canterbury Tales*.

Copley, G. J. 1971 edition *English Place Names And Their Origins*. David & Charles.

Cottle, B. 1984 edition *The Penguin Dictionary Of Surnames*. Penguin.

Dunkling, L. and Gosling, W. 1983 *Everyman's Dictionary Of First Names*. Book Club Associates.

Ekwall, E. 1960 edition *Concise Oxford Dictionary of Place Names*. Clarendon Press, Oxford.

Hassall, W. 1956 *Subsidy Roll (1305-6 and 1327), Wheatley Records (Oxon)*. Oxfordshire Record Society, Oxford.

Hassall, W. 1967 *History Through Surnames*. Pergamon Press.

Hoskins, W. G. 1967 edition *The Making Of The English Landscape*. Hodder & Stoughton.

Hughes, J. Pennethorne. 1963 *How You Got Your Name*. J.M.Dent & Sons.

Hughes, J. Pennethorne. 1967 edition *Is Thy Name Wart?* J.M.Dent & Sons.

Matthews, C. M. 1966 *English Surnames*. Weidenfield & Nicholson.

Matthews, C. M. 1967 *How Surnames Began*. Lutterworth Press.

Pine, L. G. 1965 *The Story Of Surnames*. Country Life Ltd.

Reaney, P. H. 1979 edition *The Origin of English Surnames*. Routledge & Keegan Paul, London.

Reaney, P. H. 1976 *A Dictionary of British Surnames*. Routledge & Keegan Paul, London.

Stubbs, W. 1906 edition *Constitutional History of England*. Clarendon Press.

Sweet, H. 1989 edition *Dictionary Of Anglo-Saxon*. Oxford University Press.

Tengvik, G. 1958 *Old English Bynames*. Almqvist & Wiksell, Stockholm.

Tonkeieff, O. G. 1966 *Life in Norman England* Batsford, London.

Walker, M. (Editor) 1954 *Feet of fines for the county of Lincoln for the reign of King John, 1199-1216* Pipe Roll Society, London.

Verstappen, P. 1982 edition *The Book Of Surnames*. Pelham.

Weekley, E. 1936 *Surnames*. John Murray, London.

General Index

Index of Surnames

CPSIA information can be obtained
at www.ICGtesting.com
Printed in the USA
LVHW111407030320
648851LV00011B/455/J

9 780956 510600